FTCE English for Speakers of Other Languages (ESOL) K-12

Teacher Certification Exam Guide

By: Sharon A Wynne, M.S.

XAMonline, Inc.

Boston

XAMonline, Inc.
21 Orient Avenue
Melrose, MA 02176
Toll Free 1-800-509-4128
Email: info@xamonline.com
Web: www.xamonline.com
Fax: 1-617-583-5552

Library of Congress Cataloging-in-Publication Data

Wynne, Sharon A.

FTCE English for Speakers of Other Languages (ESOL) K-12 Teacher Certification / Sharon A. Wynne. ISBN 978-1-60787-530-7

1. English for Speakers of Other Languages (ESOL)   2. Study Guides.
3. FTCE   4. Teachers' Certification & Licensure   5. Careers

Disclaimer:
The opinions expressed in this publication are solely those of XAMonline and were created independently from the National Education Association, Educational Testing Service, and any State Department of Education, National Evaluation Systems or other testing affiliates.

Between the time of publication and printing, state-specific standards as well as testing formats and website information may produce change that is not included in part or in whole within this product. Sample test questions are developed by XAMonline and reflect similar content to real tests; however, they are not former tests. XAMonline assembles content that aligns with state standards but makes no claims nor guarantees teacher candidates a passing score. Numerical scores are determined by testing companies such as NES or ETS and then are compared with individual state standards. A passing score varies from state to state.

Printed in the United States of America
FTCE English for Speakers of Other Languages (ESOL) K-12
ISBN: 978-1-60787-530-7

Florida Teacher Certification Exam (FTCE):
English for Speakers of Other Languages (ESOL) K-12

In order to obtain teacher certification in the subject area of secondary ESOL, a passing score is required on the FTCE ESOL K-12 exam. The FTCE ESOL K-12 exam is offered year-round at locations within Florida and nationwide. When registering for the test, you will select the date and location that best meets your individual needs.

Test Format: CBT

This exam is offered as a Computer-Based Test (CBT) at testing locations across the country. All tests must be completed using a designated testing center computer. You can perform a search on http://www.fl.nesinc.com/ to locate the test center that is most convenient for you.

Time: 2.5 hours

You are allotted two hours and 30 minutes to complete this exam. While there are no structured break times, you are allowed to use the restroom and take breaks throughout the testing period. Time on a break will count towards your overall testing period; in other words, the clock does not stop while you step out to take a break. You will be provided with specific break instructions by the assigned proctor at your testing location.

Question Format: Multiple-Choice

Each test has approximately 120 questions in multiple-choice format. Each competency has a percentage of questions allotted to ensure every topic is covered within the exam. You will see within this test preparation guide that each competency is broken down to a number of smaller categories, also known as skills. Using the following chart, you can see the specific breakdown for each of the 11 FTCE ESOL K-12 competencies:

Competency	% of Test Questions
Knowledge of culture as a factor in English language learners' (ELLs') learning	8%
Knowledge of language as a system	12%
Knowledge of language acquisition and development	12%
Knowledge of second language literacy development	10%
Knowledge of ESL/ESOL research, history, public policy, and current practices	5%
Knowledge of standards-based ESOL and content instruction	14%
Knowledge of resources and technologies	8%
Knowledge of planning standards-based instruction of ELLs	10%
Knowledge of assessment issues for ELLs	8%
Knowledge of language proficiency assessment	5%
Knowledge of classroom-based assessment for ELLs	8%
TOTAL	100%

Passing Score: 200

Scores are calculated using a scaled score, meaning, only your correct answers will count towards your final score. 200 points are required in order to pass this exam. There is no penalty for guessing.

TABLE OF CONTENTS

COMPETENCY 1.0   **Knowledge of culture as a factor in English language learners' (ELLs') learning** 1

Skill 1.1   Analyze elements of culture and their impact on the instruction of ELLs 1

Skill 1.2   Identify ways that student participation, learning, and behavior can be affected by cultural differences (e.g., religious, economic, social, family) 2

Skill 1.3   Identify phases and distinguish among characteristics of cultural adaptation (e.g., assimilation, acculturation) in order to better understand ELLs 3

Skill 1.4   Select a variety of resources to obtain information about the cultural background and experiences of ELLs and their families to guide curriculum development and instruction 5

Skill 1.5   Select strategies to promote multicultural sensitivity and diversity in the classroom 8

Skill 1.6   Identify ways that home/school connections build partnerships with ELLs' families (e.g., Parent Leadership Councils) 9

Skill 1.7   Analyze social issues and trends (e.g., immigration) that affect the education of ELLs 9

COMPETENCY 2.0   **Knowledge of language as a system** 11

Skill 2.1   Identify how the universal principles of language (e.g., systematic, rule-governed, arbitrary) guide ELL instruction 11

Skill 2.2   Apply principles of phonology to facilitate ELLs' English language acquisition 11

Skill 2.3   Apply principles of morphology to facilitate ELLs' English language acquisition 13

Skill 2.4   Apply principles of semantics to facilitate ELLs' English language acquisition .14

Skill 2.5   Apply principles of English pragmatics as they relate to language acquisition .15

Skill 2.6   Apply principles of syntax to facilitate ELLs' English language acquisition 15

Skill 2.7   Apply principles of English discourse (e.g., written and oral) to facilitate ELLs' English language acquisition 17

Skill 2.8   Identify and apply appropriate forms of the English language for different purposes 18

Skill 2.9   Identify phonological, morphological, semantic, pragmatic, syntactic, and discourse differences between English and other languages 21

COMPETENCY 3.0   Knowledge of language acquisition and development........22

Skill 3.1   Identify the major theories of first and second language acquisition that inform classroom practices 22

Skill 3.2   Identify and compare first and second language acquisition processes that affect student learning..24

Skill 3.3   Use research-based models of instruction including bilingual, sheltered, and/or inclusion..25

Skill 3.4   Determine characteristics of bilingualism 27

Skill 3.5   Determine the factors that influence the development of bilingualism 27

Skill 3.6   Identify how ELLs' use of home language serves as a foundation for learning English 28

Skill 3.7   Determine factors that affect ELLs' learning of English, including psychological, social, cultural, and political factors 28

Skill 3.8   Apply individual learner variables to guide the process of learning English as a Second Language 30

Skill 3.9   Distinguish characteristics of social language (e.g., basic interpersonal communication skills [BICS]) and academic language (e.g., cognitive academic language proficiency [CALP])..31

Skill 3.10   Identify sources of ELLs' errors (e.g., interlanguage) to guide effective instruction 32

Skill 3.11   Identify language functions (e.g., communicating needs, purpose, desires) of spoken and written English to facilitate English language acquisition............34

COMPETENCY 4.0   Knowledge of second language literacy development.........35

Skill 4.1   Determine and apply current theories of second language reading development for ELLs at varying English proficiency levels 35

Skill 4.2   Determine and apply current theories of second language writing development for ELLs at varying English proficiency levels 36

Skill 4.3   Identify how ELLs' L1 oral language influences the use of oral and written English in the classroom 37

Skill 4.4   Identify how ELLs' home literacy practices (e.g., oral, written) influence the development of oral and written English 38

Skill 4.5   Select methods to incorporate students' L1 literacy into English language literacy development (e.g., transfer) 39

COMPETENCY 5.0   Knowledge of ESL/ESOL research, history, public policy, and current practices..40

Skill 5.1   Identify past and present approaches to ESOL instruction (e.g., grammar-translation, audio-lingual, Communicative Language Teaching, Natural Approach, TPR, CALLA, SIOP) 40

Skill 5.2   Identify major researchers and how their contributions have affected the field of second language teaching and learning 41

Skill 5.3   Relate current research to best practices in second language and literacy instruction 43

Skill 5.4   Evaluate appropriate research-based models of instruction for ELLs 44

Skill 5.5   Identify major federal and state court decisions, laws, and policies that have affected the education of ELLs 44

Skill 5.6   Apply the sections and requirements of the *League of United Latin American Citizens (LULAC) et al. v. State Board of Education* Consent Decree, 1990 (1990 Florida Consent Decree) to specific situations. 46

COMPETENCY 6.0   Knowledge of standards-based ESOL and content instruction...**49**

Skill 6.1   Select methods to improve ELLs' English listening skills for a variety of academic and social purposes 49

Skill 6.2   Select methods to improve ELLs' English speaking skills for a variety of academic and social purposes 49

Skill 6.3   Apply standards-based instruction that develops ELLs' oral English in order to support learning in reading and writing English..50

Skill 6.4   Apply appropriate standards-based reading instruction for ELLs at varying English proficiency levels...52

Skill 6.5   Apply appropriate standards-based writing instruction for ELLs at varying English proficiency levels...55

Skill 6.6   Select methods to develop ELLs' writing through a range of activities from sentence formation to extended writing (e.g., expository, narrative, persuasion) 56

Skill 6.7   Select activities, tasks, and assignments that develop authentic uses (e.g., real-world, contextualized) of English language and literacy to assist ELLs in learning academic language and content-area material 57

Skill 6.8   Select instruction that effectively integrates listening, speaking, reading, and writing for ELLs at varying English proficiency levels..................................58

Skill 6.9   Identify appropriate adaptations of curricular materials and modifications of instruction according to an ELL's level of English proficiency and prior knowledge 59

COMPETENCY 7.0   Knowledge of resources and techniques **61**

Skill 7.1   Evaluate and select culturally responsive, age-appropriate, and linguistically accessible materials for ELLs at varying English proficiency levels 61

Skill 7.2   Evaluate and select a variety of materials and other resources, including L1 resources, appropriate to ELLs' English language and literacy development ...61

Skill 7.3   Apply technological resources (e.g., Internet, software, computers, related media) to enhance language and content-area instruction for ELLs at varying English proficiency levels..61

Skill 7.4   Identify effective means of collaboration with school-based, district, and community resources to advocate for equitable access for ELLs...................63

Skill 7.5   Identify major professional organizations, publications, and resources that support continuing education for teachers 63

COMPETENCY 8.0   Knowledge of planning standards-based instruction to ELLs..64

Skill 8.1   Apply appropriate language objectives and state-approved content-based standards to plan instruction for ELLs at varying English proficiency levels ...64

Skill 8.2   Identify the characteristics of engaging, challenging, and collaborative student-centered classroom environments for diverse learners 65

Skill 8.3   Choose appropriate differentiated learning experiences for lesson planning based on students' English proficiency levels 65

Skill 8.4   Choose appropriate learning tasks for students with limited L1 literacy and/or limited formal schooling..66

Skill 8.5   Identify methods of scaffolding and providing context for ELLs' learning....67

Skill 8.6   Identify situations in which reteaching is necessary and appropriate for ELLs ...68

COMPETENCY 9.0   Knowledge of assessment issues for ELLs 69

Skill 9.1   Identify factors such as cultural and linguistic bias that affect the assessment of ELLs 69

Skill 9.2   Evaluate formal and informal assessment to measure oral language, literacy, and academic achievement 71

Skill 9.3   Determine appropriate accommodations during formal and informal assessments of ELLs at varying English language proficiency levels.............71

Skill 9.4   Identify characteristics of ELLs with special needs (e.g., speech-language impaired, intellectual disabilities, specific learning disabilities)....................72

Skill 9.5   Distinguish between the characteristics of ELLs in the natural process of acquiring English and ELLs with specific learning disabilities 72

Skill 9.6   Identify characteristics of ELLs who are gifted and talented 73

COMPETENCY 10.0   Knowledge of language proficiency assessment..................75

Skill 10.1   Identify the district, state, and federal requirements for identification, reclassification, and exit of ELLs from ESOL programs 75

Skill 10.2   Interpret assessment data from multiple sources to guide instruction for ELLs at varying English proficiency levels...76

Skill 10.3   Identify effective ways to communicate with stakeholders (e.g., primary caregivers, school and district staff, community members) about assessment outcomes that guide policy and instructional practice.....................................77

COMPETENCY 11.0   Knowledge of classroom-based assessment for ELLs 78

Skill 11.1   Identify appropriate use of alternative assessments (e.g., authentic, performance-based, peer- and self-assessments) to evaluate content-area learning for ELLs at varying English proficiency levels 78

Skill 11.2   Identify appropriate measurement concepts (e.g., reliability, validity), test characteristics, and uses of norm-referenced and criterion-referenced assessments in evaluating ELLs..78

Skill 11.3   Use a variety of instruments (e.g., portfolios, checklists, rubrics, anecdotal records) to assess students as they perform authentic tasks (e.g., real-world, contextualized)...79

Skill 11.4   Identify appropriate test-taking skills and strategies needed by ELLs 80

Skill 11.5   Determine appropriate modifications of classroom tests, including test items and tasks, for ELLs at varying English proficiency levels 80

GLOSSARY OF ABBREVIATIONS AND ACRONYMS 82

BIBLIOGRAPHY 84

SAMPLE TEST 91

ANSWER KEY 117

RATIONALES 118

COMPETENCY 1.0   **Knowledge of culture as a factor in English language learners' (ELLs') learning**

Skill 1.1   **Analyze elements of culture and their impact on the instruction of ELLs**

While there is a continuous effort to establish a Standard English to be taught for English Language Learners (ELLs), English learning and acquisition depends on the cultural and linguistic background of the ELL and on preconceived perceptions of English language cultural influences. These factors can act as a filter, causing confusion and inhibiting learning. Since language by definition is an attempt to share knowledge, the cultural, ethnic, and linguistic diversity of learners influences both their own history and how they approach and learn a new language.

Teachers must assess the ELL to determine how cultural, ethnic, and linguistic experience can impact the student's learning. This evaluation should take into account many factors, including

- the cultural background and educational sophistication of the ELL; and
- the exposure of the ELL to various English language variants and cultural beliefs.

No single approach, program, or set of practices fit all students' needs, backgrounds, and experiences. The ideal program for a Native American teenager attending an isolated tribal school may fail to reach a Hispanic youth enrolled in an inner-city or suburban district.

Customs play an important part in language learning because they directly affect interpersonal exchanges. What is polite in one culture might be offensive in another. For example, in the United States, making direct eye contact is considered polite and avoiding eye contact connotes deviousness, inattention, or rude behavior; however, the custom in many Asian cultures is the opposite. Teachers who are unaware of this cultural difference can offend an Asian ELL and unwittingly cause a barrier to learning. However, teachers who are familiar with this custom can make efforts to avoid offending the learner and can teach the difference between the two customs so that the ELL can learn how to interact without allowing contrary customs to interfere.

Beliefs and institutions have a strong emotional influence on ELLs and always should be respected. Although customs should be adaptable, like switching registers when speaking, teachers should not attempt to change the beliefs or institutional values of an ELL. Presenting new ideas is a part of growth, learning, and understanding. Even though the beliefs and values of different cultures often have irreconcilable differences, the teacher should address them. In these instances, teachers must respect alternative attitudes and adopt an "agree to disagree" attitude. Presenting new, contrasting points of view should not be avoided because new ideas can both strengthen and change original thinking. All presentations should be neutral, however, and no effort should be made to alter a learner's thinking. While addressing individual cultural differences, teachers also should teach tolerance of all cultures. This is especially important in a culturally diverse classroom, but will serve all students well in their future interactions.

Studying the **history and various art forms** of cultures reveals much about a culture and offers opportunities to tap into the interests and talents of ELLs. Comparing the history and art of different cultures encourages critical thinking and often reveals commonalities as well as differences, which leads to greater understanding among people.

Culture is a rich component of language learning. It offers a means of drawing learners into the learning process and greatly expands their understanding of both the new culture and their own. Second language acquisition, according to the findings of Saville-Troike (1986), places the learner in the position of having to learn a second culture. Learning a second culture can have negative or positive results, depending not only on how teaching is approached but also on outside factors. How people in the new culture respond to ELLs makes them feel welcome or rejected. The attitudes and behavior of the learner's family are particularly important. If the family is supportive and embraces the second culture, then the effect is typically positive. However, if acculturation is perceived as rejecting the primary culture, then the child risks feeling alienated from both cultures.

| Skill 1.2 | Identify ways that student participation, learning, and behavior can be affected by cultural differences (e.g., religious, economic, social, family) |

There are many different ways that students are affected by the cultural differences between their native culture and home and the culture they are acquiring through schooling and daily life in a foreign culture.

The following points, adapted from Peregoy and Boyle (2008), illustrate some of the many different ways that culture affects us daily and thus affect students in their participation, learning, and adjustment to a different society and its schools:

- **Family structures:** What constitutes a family? What are the rights and responsibilities of each family member? What is the hierarchy of authority?

- **Life cycles:** What are the criteria for defining stages, periods, or transitions in life? What rites of passage are there? What behaviors are considered appropriate for children of different ages? How might these conflict with behaviors taught or encouraged in school?

- **Roles and interpersonal relationships:** How do the roles of girls and women differ from those of boys and men? How do people greet each other? Do girls work and interact with boys? Is deference shown? If so, to whom and by whom?

- **Discipline:** What is discipline? Which behaviors are considered socially acceptable for boys versus girls at different ages? Who or what is considered responsible if a child misbehaves? The child? Parents? Older siblings? The environment? Is blame even ascribed? Who has authority over whom? How is behavior traditionally controlled? To what extent and in what domains?

- **Time and space:** How important is punctuality? How important is speed in completing a task? How much space are people accustomed to? What significance is associated with different cultural locations or directions, including north, south, east, and west?

- **Religion:** What restrictions are there on topics discussed in school? Are dietary restrictions, including fasting, to be observed? What restrictions are associated with death and the dead?

- **Food:** What is eaten? In what order and how often is food eaten? Which foods are restricted? Which foods are typical? What social obligations are there with regard to food giving, reciprocity, and honoring people? What restrictions or proscriptions are associated with handling, offering, or discarding food?

- **Health and hygiene:** How are illnesses treated, and by whom? What is considered the cause? If a student were involved in an accident at school, would any of the common first aid practices be unacceptable?

- **History, traditions, and holidays:** Which events and people are sources of pride for this group? To what extent does the group in the United States identify with the history and traditions of the country of origin? What holidays and celebrations are considered appropriate for observing in school? Which ones are appropriate for private observance?

Skill 1.3	**Identify phases and distinguish among characteristics of cultural adaptation (e.g., assimilation, acculturation) in order to better understand ELLs**

Culture concerns the shared beliefs, values, and rule-governed patterns of behavior, including language, that define a group and are required for group membership (Goodenough 1981; Saville-Troike 1978). Cultural adjustment occurs when people from different cultures are subjected to changes in their beliefs, habits, and customs. These changes may come because the person has had to flee his or her country or leave it permanently. In an effort to seek better educational, financial, or cultural opportunities, many others choose to leave their native land and become part of a foreign culture.

There are four generally recognized stages of acculturation:

- **The Honeymoon Stage:** Everything looks bright and positive. The individuals or families have arrived in their new land and are ready to begin a new era in their life. Everyone is eager to please, ready to interact, and happy to be in their new home.

- **The Hostility Stage:** Frustration begins to occur as reality strikes. The new language, the new survival tasks (dealing with subways or buses), new foods, and new ways of doing things (at work or at school) are unfamiliar and viewed as problems with the new society. Depression, anger, anxiety, and homesickness are felt during this phase.

- **The Humor Stage:** Accomplishments bring a triumphant feeling that the new society might not be so bad. As the individuals or families experience success and adjust to life's new demands, they are able to laugh at themselves and their previous frustrations.

- **The Home Stage:** The individuals or families retain patriotism to their native country while accepting the new country as their new home. A transition from the old to the new norms has occurred, and the new location is seen as home.

The duration of each stage depends on the individual and may be shortened by positive experiences within the individual's circle of contacts. At its most basic level, cultural adaptation generally is considered to be assimilation and acculturation, though social anthropologists have many more definitions to describe the complex phenomena of cultures coming together.

Assimilation is the process of integration of immigrants or minorities into the predominate culture. This implies immigrants or minorities lose their native culture through loss of language, customs, ethnicity, and self-identity.

The "Melting Pot Theory" was an attempt to explain the assimilation process in the United States when it was assumed that the United States was an ideal homogeneous society in which cultural differences, except physical ones such as skin color, were ignored. This utopian vision of the United States has led to other metaphors such as "vegetable soup" or "flower garden" to explain the trend toward a more pluralistic society in recent years.

Social scientists use four benchmarks to evaluate the degree of social assimilation: socioeconomic status, geographic distribution, second language attainment, and intermarriage. The degree to which the immigrants or minorities achieve socioeconomic status through education, jobs, and income mark the degree of assimilation. As it becomes assimilated by increased socioeconomic attainment, longer residency in the United States, and higher generational status, the immigrant culture seems to spread out and move away from intense geographic concentration. Language assimilation is considered to be a three-generation process. The first generation tries to learn the new language, but the native tongue remains dominant; the second generation is bilingual; and the third generation loses their "native" language, speaking only the language of the new country. High rates of intermarriage are presumed to be strong indicators of social integration because intermarriage reduces the ability for a family to pass on one consistent culture and therefore becomes an agent of assimilation.

Acculturation occurs when two distinct cultures come in contact, altering the original cultural patterns of either or both groups, but the cultural groups remain distinct. Definitions and evidence of acculturation state that this is a two-way process, but research and theory continue to explore the adjustments and changes that aboriginal peoples, immigrants, and other minorities experience when in contact with the dominant culture. Thus, acculturation is believed to be the process by which cultural learning is imposed upon the weaker cultures simply because they are weaker. Acculturation then becomes a process of learning a second culture, and the minorities' culture becomes displaced. Transculturation is acculturation by an individual; acculturation is by a large group.

Skill 1.4 **Select a variety of resources to obtain information about the cultural background and experiences of ELLs and their families to guide curriculum development and instruction**

The State of Florida has in place several unique resources that help teachers address cultural, ethnic, and linguistic differences among their students. Among the resources available to teachers is the Florida Language Arts Curriculum Framework, which was developed to enhance the Language Arts Curriculum Framework and ensure that the goals of the Florida School Improvement and Accountability Initiative are met.

The **Parent Leadership Council** is a council set up in each school that allows parents to be involved in and participate in educational programming for their children. A majority of the parents on the council must be parents of LEP students. The council must be consulted before the LEP district plan is submitted to the state for approval.

The **LEP committee** is a committee of ESOL teacher(s), the home language teacher (if any), an administrator (or designee), plus guidance counselor(s), social worker(s), school psychologist(s), or other educators as needed for the situation. The parents also are encouraged to attend the meetings of the committee.

Organizations provide additional resources supplying help to educators of ELLs:

 • **Teachers of English to Speakers of Other Languages** and its regional affiliates.
www.tesol.org

• **Bilingual Association of Florida**
Oneyda M. Paneque, Ed.D.
Miami Dade College
InterAmerican Campus
School of Education
627 SW 27th Ave.
Miami, FL 33135
Phone: 305-237-6707; Fax: 305-237-6179
opaneque@mdc.edu

• **Florida Association for Bilingual Education Supervisors (FABES)**
Dr. Margarita Pinkos, President
Palm Beach County Public Schools
ESOL/Multicultural Department
3388 Forest Hill Blvd., Suite A 204
West Palm Beach, FL 33411
Phone: 561-434-8010; Fax: 561-644-5942
margarita.pinkos@palmbeachschools.org

• **Center for Applied Linguistics.** www.cal.org

- **U.S. Department of Education's Office of English Language Acquisition Language Enhancement, and Academic Achievement for Limited English Proficient Students (OELA).** www2.ed.gov/about/offices/list/OELA/index.html

Books and journals offer supplemental resources for addressing cultural, ethnic, and linguistic differences. These are among the noteworthy:

- **Beebe, Von N., and William F. Mackey.** *Bilingual Schooling and the Miami Experience.* Coral Gables: Institute of Interamerican Studies. Graduate School of International Studies. University of Miami, 1990. Extensively documents the influx of Cuban refugees into the Miami-Dade County school system.
- **TESOL Journal**
- **Bilingual Research Journal**

Several websites provide additional resources for teachers of ELLs:

English Language Learner Knowledge Base
www.helpforschools.com/ELLKBase/index.shtml
- Valuable for the latest information on ELLs, including conferences, program evaluations, legislation, parental outreach, and a database. Also see SOLOM at www.helpforschools.com/ELLKBase/forms/SOLOM.shtml.

WebQuests
http://webquest.sdsu.edu
- WebQuests support teachers with a scaffold for organizing theme-based research units by using the Internet as a learning tool and source of information.

General Resources Available on the Web

Besides their specific charge, these offices generally include information on ESL/bilingual educational issues, documents, and teaching resources of concern to educators across the nation. A multitude of organizations are dedicated to providing quality education for the English Language Learner. The following websites are among the many available to support teachers and help them keep up to date with the latest research in the field of English Language Learning.

California Department of Education. http://www.cde.ca.gov/sp/el/

Center for Applied Linguistics. http://www.cal.org

Center for Multilingual, Multicultural Research. http://www-rcf.usc.edu/~cmmr/

ERIC Clearinghouse on Language and Linguistics. http://eric.ed.gov

Kristina Pfaff's Linguistic Funland. http://www.linguistic-funland.com/

National Association for Bilingual Education. http://www.nabe.org/

National Clearinghouse for Bilingual Education. http://www.ncela.us

Northwest Regional Educational Laboratory. http://www.nwrel.org/

Office of Superintendent of Public Instruction (OSPI), Washington State. http://www.k12.wa.us/

Teachers of English to Speakers of other Languages, Inc. http://www.tesol.edu/index.html

The Office for Civil Rights (OCR). www2.ed.gov/about/offices/list/ocr/index.html

The U.S. Department of Education. http://www.ed.gov/

The U.S. Department of Education, Office of English Language Acquisition, Language Enhancement and Academic Achievement for Limited English Proficient Students (OELA). http://www2.ed.gov/about/offices/list/oela/index.html

The Institute of Education Services. http://www2.ed.gov/about/offices/list/ies/index.html

The U.S. Department of Education, Office of Educational Research and Improvement (OERI). http://www.ed.gov/offices/OERI/

University of Texas at Austin, College of Education. http://www.edb.utexas.edu/education/centers/obe/

In addition to these resources for teachers and administrators, websites are available for students to practice their ELL skills. There are two of the most popular:

About.com: ESL: This popular site has exercises in all four skills, games, and quizzes for ELLs and information for teachers. http://www.esl.about.com

Dave's ESL Café: One of the longest-running websites with sections for students, teachers, and job seekers. http://www.eslcafe.com/

Skill 1.5   **Select strategies to promote multicultural sensitivity and diversity in the classroom**

Teachers are both participants and observers in their classrooms. As such, they are in a unique position to observe what makes their students uncomfortable. By writing these observations in a teaching journal, the teacher can begin to note what activities and topics make the students in his or her classroom uncomfortable. Does this discomfort come from multicultural insensitivity?

One method of demonstrating sensitivity is to use appropriate "teacher talk" in the classroom. "Wait time" for student responses differs with different cultures. Also, students who are struggling to formulate their answers may need more time than the teacher normally gives for responding. Also, if the questions are rhetorical, students may be reluctant to answer them because they see no point to such questions.

Cooperative group work is based on the premise that many cultures are more comfortable working in collaborative groups. Although this is true, many students may feel that the teacher is the only academic authority in the classroom and, as such, should answer questions, not their peers. Different students feel more comfortable with different instructional formats. This may be due to both cultural and individual preferences. By balancing group work with teacher-directed instruction, teachers can accommodate both points of view.

Literacy and reading instruction are areas in which multicultural sensitivity can be increased in the classroom regardless of the level of the students. Many immigrant children arrive in the classroom with few, if any, literacy skills. They may not have had the opportunity to go to school. Others may have been fully immersed in literature and have had substantial prior education. In both cases, culturally sensitive reading materials are necessary for the students, both native English speakers and ELLs, to have the opportunity to discuss the ways in which different cultures are both alike and different. Oral discussions of the books will provide opportunities for comprehensible input and negotiation of meaning. Research has shown that the key to any reading program is extensive reading (Day and Bamford 1998; Krashen 1993). Advantages include building vocabulary and background knowledge, interest in reading, and improved comprehension.

For the multicultural classroom, it is important to provide culturally sensitive materials. Keep an eye out for materials that distort or omit certain historical events; portray stereotyping; contain loaded words; use speech that is culturally inaccurate; portray gender roles, elders, and family inaccurately; or distort or offend a student's self-image. All materials should be of high literary quality.

Show and Tell is another strategy for raising multicultural sensitivity. Students of all ages can bring in objects from their home culture and tell the class about their uses, where they are from, how they are made, and so on.

Misunderstandings can be worked into the classroom by asking students to share an incident that involved a cultural misunderstanding. Teachers can ask questions about the nature of the misunderstanding and what was involved—words, body language, social customs, or stereotypes.

Skill 1.6   **Identify ways that home/school connections build partnerships with ELLs' families (e.g., Parent Leadership Councils)**

Parent Leadership Councils (PLC) are an outcome of the Florida Consent Decree of 1990. In these councils, parent groups become involved and participate in their child's education and academic achievement at each school or at the district level. Most of these parental groups consist of parents of LEP/ELL students who promote the welfare of the LEP/ELL in school, at home, and in the community.

A major function of the group is to monitor the DOE/META Agreement in its school district and ensure that the rights of and services to LEP/ELL comply with the Consent Decree. Such councils frequently meet once a month with school leaders in an effort to develop positive, professional relationships among administrators, teachers, and parents. During such meetings, parents are informed about and become involved in their child's education.

Depending on the school district and needs, parents may be provided with leadership training and orientation to the district's LEP program monitoring and involvement procedures. They may be represented on existing school and district advisory committees.

Parents who wish to serve on the leadership council in their school district should contact the ESOL Teacher or Principal for assistance.

Skill 1.7   **Analyze social issues and trends (e.g., immigration) that affect the education of ELLs**

According to the Pew Research Center, immigrants arriving in the United States from 2005 to 2050 will account for 82 percent of the U.S. population growth. This means that a large number of Americans will either not speak fluent English or speak it as a second language. Currently, only 23 percent of first-generation immigrants speak fluent English, compared with 88 percent of second-generation immigrants and 94 percent of third-generation immigrants. An increasing number of first-generation immigrants will put increased demands on second language programs.

Racial relations have become strained, especially between the two largest minority groups: African Americans and Latinos. Anti-immigration attitudes often arise from the belief that immigrants reduce job opportunities. Within individual schools, the two groups have distinct cultures that typically remain separate. When schools offer activities, such as sports, multicultural celebrations, and other activities that transcend cultural differences, they reduce the emphasis on difference and allow students to recognize their commonalities.

The increase in gang activity already has begun to affect the education of ELLs. Gangs lure ELLs away from school because they offer acceptance and opportunities (often illegal) to earn more money than students could otherwise earn.

Communities that embrace multiculturalism are able to reduce the isolation of individual ethnic groups and promote healthy intercultural relations. All over the country, the influence of other cultures has increased. For example, food from a large range of cultures is now available nearly everywhere. In a small geographic area, one might encounter Mexican, Middle Eastern, African, French, German, and Spanish restaurants. Increased globalization has brought products and customs from all over the world to the United States and created greater cultural awareness. When people more readily accept cultural differences, their willingness to socialize with and help ELLs increases.

Unfortunately, the events of 9/11 caused a major setback, particularly for Middle Easterners and Muslims. Many people jumped to unjustified conclusions and condemned others based on untrue generalizations or stereotypes. Gradually, these unfortunate attitudes have been replaced by more realistic perceptions. However, restrictions on foreign students have continued to limit the number of students from other countries who can or are willing to study in the United States.

Anti-immigration sentiments also have caused problems for ELLs. Although public schools cannot discriminate based on citizenship, many students live in fear that they or members of their family will be deported. Congress repeatedly has tried to address this problem but so far has not resolved it.

COMPETENCY 2.0   **Knowledge of language as a system**

Skill 2.1   **Identify how the universal principles of language (e.g., systematic, rule-governed, arbitrary) guide ELL instruction**

According to the *Oxford Companion to the English Language*, language is a system in which the basic rules are assembled according to a basic set of rules. There are two major divisions of language: natural language and artificial language. In natural language, humans use language in a traditional way. Esperanto is a devised language that Ludwig Lazarus Zamenhof derived from Romance and Germanic languages in the hopes that it would become the most popular language in the world. A computer language such as COBOL is used to interface with computers.

Human communication is multimodal because speech, gesture, writing, touch, and so on interact. Language has the following properties:

- A vocal-auditory channel: sounds are produced by the vocal cords and received by the auditory canal.
- Convertibility to other media: writing and print (the graphic medium), sign language (a visual medium), braille (a tactile medium).
- Use of arbitrary symbols: symbols usually are unrelated to meaning.
- Duality or double articulation: units of sound do not have meaning in most cases but are combined with other units that do.
- Interdependence: Language is an integrated structure in which the role of all items is defined by all other items in the same language.
- Open-endedness: the number of utterances is infinitely large and depend on productivity and creativity
- Displacement: Language is used to recount events irrespective of time or place or of whether or not they existed.
- Continual change
- Turn-taking

(Adapted from the *Oxford Companion to the English Language*)

Skill 2.2   **Apply principles of phonology to facilitate ELLs' English language acquisition**

Phonology can be defined as the way in which speech sounds form patterns (Díaz-Rico and Weed 1995). Phonology is a subset of the linguistics field, which studies the organization and systems of sound within a particular language. Phonology is based on the theory that every native speaker unconsciously retains the sound structure of that language and is more concerned with the sounds than with the physical process of creating those sounds.

When babies babble or make what we call "baby talk", they are actually experimenting with all of the sounds represented in all languages. As they learn a specific language, they become more proficient in the sounds of that language and forget how to make sounds that they don't need or use.

Phonemes, pitch, and stress are all components of phonology. Because each affects the meaning of communications, they are variables that ELLs must recognize and learn.

Phonology analyzes the sound structure of the given language by

- determining which phonetic sounds have the most significance; and
- explaining how these sounds influence a native speaker of the language.

For example, the Russian alphabet has a consonant that, when pronounced, sounds like the word "rouge" in French. English speakers typically have difficulty pronouncing this sound pattern because inherently they know this is not a typical English sound, even though they occasionally encounter it (Díaz-Rico and Weed 1995).

Mastering a sound that does not occur in the learner's first language requires repetition, both of hearing the sound and of attempting to say it. The older the learner, the more difficult this becomes, especially if the learner has spoken only one language before reaching puberty. Correct pronunciation may require years of practice because the learner initially may not hear the sound correctly. Expecting an ELL to master a foreign pronunciation quickly leads to frustration for the teacher and the learner. With enough focused repetition, however, the learner eventually may hear the difference and then be able to imitate it. Inadequate listening and speaking practice will result in a persistent heavy accent.

Phonemes are the smallest unit of sound that affects meaning—that is, distinguishes words from one another. In English, there are approximately 44 speech sounds but only 26 letters, so the sounds, when combined, become words. For this reason, English is not considered a phonetic language where there is a one-to-one correspondence between letters and sounds. For example, consider the two words "pin" and "bin." The only difference is the first consonant of the words, the "p" in "pin" and "b" in "bin." This makes the sounds "p" and "b" phonemes in English, because the difference in sound creates a difference in meaning.

Focusing on phonemes to provide pronunciation practice allows students to have fun while they learn to recognize and say sounds. Pairs or groups of words that have a set pattern make learning easier. For example, students can practice saying or thinking of words that rhyme but begin with a different phoneme, such as tan, man, fan, and ran. Other groups of words start with the same phoneme followed by various vowel sounds, such as ten, ton, tan, and tin. This kind of alliteration can be expanded into tongue twisters that students find challenging and fun.

Pitch in communication determines the context or meaning of a word or a series of words. A string of words can communicate more than one meaning, for example, when posed as a question or statement. For example, the phrase "I can't go" is a statement if the pitch or intonation falls. However, the same phrase becomes the question "I can't go?" if the pitch or intonation rises for the word "go."

Stress can occur at a word or sentence level. At the word level, placing the stress on a different syllable can modify the word's meaning. Consider the word "conflict." To pronounce it as a noun, one would stress the first syllable: "CONflict." However, to use it as a verb, one would stress the second syllable: "conFLICT."

Different dialects sometimes pronounce the same word differently, even though both pronunciations have the same meaning. For example, in some parts of the United States the word "insurance" is pronounced by stressing the second syllable, while in other parts of the country the first syllable is stressed.

Skill 2.3   **Apply principles of morphology to facilitate ELLs' English language acquisition**

Morphology refers to the process of how the words of a language are formed to create meaningful messages. ESOL teachers need to be aware of the principles of morphology in English to provide meaningful activities that will help in the process of language acquisition.

ESOL learners need to understand the structure of words in English and how words can be created and altered. The following are some underlying principles of the morphology of English:

1. Morphemes may be free and able to stand by themselves (e.g., chair, bag) or they may be bound or derivational, needing to be used with other morphemes to create meaning (e.g., read-able, en-able).
2. Knowledge of the meanings of derivational morphemes such as prefixes and suffixes enables students to decode word meanings and create words in the language through word analysis (e.g., un-happy means not happy).
3. Some morphemes in English provide grammatical rather than semantic information to words and sentences (e.g., of, the, and).
4. Words can be combined in English to create new compound words (e.g., key + chain = keychain).

ESOL teachers also need to be aware that principles of morphology from the student's native language may be transferred and either promote or interfere with the second language learning process.

When students overgeneralize a learned rule or simply make a mistake, teachers should make corrections in a way that does not embarrass the student. Teachers also must consider a student's stage of progress and the context of the error. Correcting every error is unnecessary when students are experimenting with language and bravely trying to use a language they are struggling to learn. A useful technique is to repeat segments of spoken language, as if to confirm understanding, and correct any errors. This saves face for the student and allows the teacher to demonstrate the correct word use or pronunciation. If the student fails to notice the correction and makes the same error again, the teacher can repeat the same type of correction. Teachers also can demonstrate variations of words in this manner, such as using a different verb tense to paraphrase what was said.

Constantly interrupting speech to make corrections or correcting every error in a writing sample can discourage participation and cause students to shut down to learning. Keeping track of errors that students repeat allows the teacher to reteach specific skills or address specific needs, either with a group of students who all need to master that skill or individually with a student who has not yet mastered a skill after others in the class have.

Skill 2.4   **Apply principles of semantics to facilitate ELLs' English language acquisition**

Semantics encompasses the meaning of individual words and combinations of words. Native speakers have used their language to function in their daily lives at all levels. Through experience they know the effects of intonation, connotation, and synonyms. This is not true of foreign speakers. In an ESOL class, instructors are trying to teach what the native speaker already knows as quickly as possible. The objectives of beginning ESOL lesson plans should deliberately build a foundation that will enable students to meet more advanced objectives.

Teaching within a specific context helps students understand the meaning of words and sentences. When students can remember the context in which they learn words and recall how the words were used, they retain that knowledge and can use it when they encounter different applications of the same words.

Using words in a variety of contexts helps students reach a deeper understanding of the words. They can then guess at new meanings that are introduced in different contexts. For example, the word "conduct" can be taught in the context of *conducting* a meeting or an investigation. Later, the word "conductor" can be used in various contexts that demonstrate some similarity but have distinctly different uses of the word, such as a *conductor* of electricity; the *conductor* of a train; the *conductor* of an orchestra; and so forth.

Second language learners must learn to translate words and sentences that they already understand in their primary language into the language they wish to acquire. This can be a daunting task because of the many ways meaning is created in English. Voice inflection, variations of meaning, variations of usage, and emphasis are some of the factors that affect meaning. The lexicon of language includes the stored meaning, contextual meaning from word association, knowledge of pronunciation and grammar, and morphemes.

Idioms, particularly those that cannot be translated literally, present a particular challenge to ELLs. Here, again, creating context facilitates learning. Grouping idioms according to types of language use helps. Some idioms rely on synonyms, some hyperbole, others metaphor. Having students translate idioms from their native language into English strengthens their ability to appreciate the meaning of idioms. Also, having students create their own original idioms increases understanding.

How idioms are taught affects how well students remember them and the level of frustration these students experience. Visual representations of idioms clarify meaning and provide a memory cue to prompt recall. Using commercially produced illustrations or having students draw their own representation of the meaning makes learning idioms easier and more fun. Students also can write stories or perform skits that illustrate the meaning of idioms.

Skill 2.5 **Apply principles of English pragmatics as they relate to language acquisition**

Pragmatics is the study of how the context impacts the interpretation of language. Situations dictate language choice, body language, the degree of intimacy, and how meaning is interpreted. For example, when customers walk into bar and sit down on a stool, they expect a bartender will ask them several questions, including: "What would you like to drink?" and "Would you like to start a tab?" This sequence of events and cues is a typical pattern of interaction in a bar. Pragmatic knowledge provides the customer with a set of expectations for the flow of events. Typically people in a bar expect a certain level of social exchange that allows congeniality without intrusiveness. They expect to receive a certain level of service and to use a particular level of manners. These types of exchanges are fairly universal in bars but would be completely inappropriate in a more formal setting—for example, when conversing with the president of a corporation.

In the ESL classroom, pragmatics can be illustrated and practiced by repeating the same situation in different contexts. For example, students can write or act out how they would explain why they failed a test to three different people: their best friend, their teacher, and their parent. With a little imagination, different scenarios can be chosen that pique student interest and make learning fun. For example, explain an embarrassing event in different contexts, such as in front of a boy/girl you want to impress, a close friend, and an authority figure. For students with very low language skills, pantomime can encourage participation, teach the concept, and set up an opportunity for using language to describe what has happened.

Comparing the customs of various cultures provides another opportunity for illustrating how context affects meaning, especially when students in a class represent a variety of cultures. For example, in other parts of the world, especially parts of Europe and the Middle East, people commonly greet each other by kissing on both cheeks, even if meeting for the first time. However, in the United States and many other countries, this greeting is not practiced and often is considered unacceptable. For some people, this practice would be offensive or might be ridiculed. Describing and comparing cultural practices provide language practice and demonstrates meaning in context.

Explaining the nuances of English requires ongoing reinforcement. As examples surface, they should be explained and alternative ways to express the same message should be explored to clarify or expand on the meaning. Pragmatic features in communication can be indirect. For example, when parents say to their children, "Have you finished your homework?" they are implying a command that if homework has not been completed, the children should stop their current activity and finish their homework. The pragmatic features are found in what was actually said and in what was not said. Students can generate their own questions that have farther-reaching implications.

Skill 2.6 **Apply principles of syntax to facilitate ELLs' English language acquisition**

Syntax involves the order in which words are arranged to create meaning. Different languages use different patterns for sentence structure. Syntax also refers to the rules for creating correct sentence patterns. English, like many other languages, is a subject-verb-object (SVO) language, which means that in most sentences the subject precedes the verb and the object follows the verb. ELLs whose native language follows an SVO sentence structure will find it easier to master English syntax.

Language acquisition is a gradual, hierarchical, and cumulative process. This means that learners must go through and master each stage in sequence, much as Piaget theorized for learning in general. In terms of syntax, this means learners must acquire specific grammatical structures, first recognizing the difference between subject and predicate; then putting subject before predicate; and next learning more complex variations, such as questions, negatives, and relative clauses.

Although learners much pass through each stage and accumulate the language skills learned in each, learners use different approaches to mastering these skills. Some learners use more cognitive processing procedures, which means their learning takes place more through thought processes. Other learners tend to use psycholinguistic procedures. By doing so, they learn more through speaking.

Regardless of how learners process information, they all must proceed through the same stages, from the least to the most complicated.

Experts disagree on the exact definition of the phases, but a set of six general stages includes the following:

Stage of Development	**Examples**
1. Single words	I; throw; ball
2. SVO structure	I throw the ball.
3. Wh- fronting	Where are you?
Do fronting	Do you like me?
Adverb fronting	Today I go to school.
Negative + verb	She is not nice.
4. Y/N inversion	Do you know him? Yes, I know him.
Copula (linking v) inversion	Is he at school?
Particle shift	Take your hat off.
5. Do 2nd	Why did she leave?
Aux 2nd	Where has he gone?
Neg do 2nd	She does not live here.
6. Cancel inversion	I asked what she was doing.

Each progressive step requires the learner to use both knowledge from the previous step and new knowledge of the language. As ELLs progress to more advanced stages of syntax, they may react differently depending on their ability to acquire the new knowledge that is required for mastery. They progress more rapidly through the stages than they did when learning their native language.

Skill 2.7   **Apply principles of English discourse (e.g., written and oral) to facilitate ELLs' English language acquisition**

The term *discourse* refers to linguistic units composed of several sentences and is derived from the concept of discursive formation, or communication that involves specialized knowledge of various kinds. Conversations, arguments, and speeches are types of discourse. Discourse shapes the way language is transmitted and also how we organize our thoughts.

The structure of discourse varies among languages and traditions. For example, Japanese writing does not present the main idea at the beginning of an essay; rather, writing builds up to the main idea, which is presented or implied at the end of the essay. This is different from most English writing, which typically presents the main idea or thesis at the beginning of an essay and repeats it at the end.

In addition to language and structure, the topic or focus affects the discourse. The discourse in various disciplines, such as feminist studies, cultural studies, and literary theory, approaches topics differently. Discourse plays a role in all spoken and written language, and it affects our thinking. Discourse between speakers of English requires knowledge of certain protocols in addition to other aspects of language. Speakers should have the necessary skills to maintain the momentum of a conversation and to correct misunderstandings. Typical spoken discourse follows predictable patterns. For example, one person might say, "I saw a good movie last night." The other person would ask, "What was it about?" The first person then would answer in a paragraph with a topic sentence, "It was about a bunch of guys who devised a plan to rob a casino," and then proceed to fill in the details.

Vocal discourse varies significantly depending on context. People speak in different registers depending on whom they are talking to and what the occasion calls for. A candidate who is running for president will use more formal speech when speaking to a group than when having a casual conversation. The message conveyed may also vary, depending on whether the group is comprised of supporters or of people who hold different political views. In either case, the candidate must make choices about how to organize what he or she says to ensure comprehension and to hold the audience's interest.

ELLs initially might practice set conversations to learn the patterns of English discourse. Practicing in pairs and using a question and answer format gives both participants an opportunity to learn the structures of discourse and information about the other person and/or the other person's culture. Such practice also gives students practice with other language skills and can increase vocabulary. The teacher may provide a set of questions, and learners can alternate asking and answering. Short skits that repeat a limited number of words can also provide helpful practice. In addition, allowing students time to converse informally, possibly using suggested topics, reinforces speech patterns.

Polite discourse includes what is called "empty language," or perfunctory speech that has little meaning but is important in social exchanges. Frequently English speakers start a conversation by asking, "How are you?" even though they have no real interest in the other person's health. An appropriate response would be "fine," even if the responder does not feel well. The exchange is simply a polite means of starting a conversation. Likewise, at the end of a discourse empty language is frequently employed: "It was good to see you." "Good to see you, too." This type of discourse is considered part of BICS, or basic interpersonal communication skills, which learners must acquire to function in social situations. It generally is less demanding than CALP, or cognitive academic language proficiency, and it allows learners to participate in informal discourses.

Written discourse ranges from the most basic grouping of sentences to the most complicated essays and stories. Regardless of the level, English writing demands certain structure patterns. A typical paragraph begins with a topic sentence, which directly or indirectly states the focus of the paragraph; adds supporting ideas and details; and ends with a concluding sentence that relates to the focus and either states the final thought on that topic or provides a transition to the next paragraph when there are multiple paragraphs. As with spoken discourse, organization, tone, and word choice are critical to transferring thoughts successfully and maintaining interest.

As skills increase, paragraphs are combined into stories or essays. Each type of writing has specific components and structures. Story writing requires setting, plot, and character. Initially, following a chronological order is probably easiest for ELLs, but as learners become more skillful, they should practice other types of order, such as adding descriptions in spatial order.

Teachers frequently rely on the proverbial three- or five-paragraph essay to teach essay writing because it provides a rigid structure for organizing and expanding ideas within a single focus. It organizationally mirrors the paragraph structure in that the first, introductory paragraph provides the main idea or focus of the essay; each body paragraph adds and develops a supporting idea and details; and the concluding paragraph provides a summary or other type of conclusion that relates to the main idea or focus stated in the first paragraph. Obviously no one considers such mechanical essays to be the ultimate goal of essay writing. However, especially for ELLs, having a rigid structure teaches the basic organizational concept of English essays. By offering strictly defined limits, the teacher reduces the number of variables to learn about essay writing. Starting with a blank page can be overwhelming for ELLs. Working within this structure enables learners to focus on developing each paragraph, a challenging enough task when one considers the language skills required. As learners become better able to control their writing and sustain a focus, variations can be introduced and topics expanded.

Language proficiency requires both BICS and CALP. Although they have clear distinctions, they also have underlying similarities that contribute to overall language learning. In addition, students should recognize CUP, or Common Underlying Proficiency. These are skills, ideas, and concepts that learners can transfer from their first language to their English learning. Both similarities and differences between languages can help learners comprehend and learn aspects of English.

Skill 2.8   Identify and apply appropriate forms of the English language for different purposes

American English usage is influenced by the social and regional situation of its users. Linguists have found that speakers adapt their pronunciation, vocabulary, grammar, and sentence structure depending on the social situation. For example, the decision to use "-ing" or "-in" at the end of a present participle depends on the formality of the situation. Speakers talking with their friends will often drop the "g" and use "in" to signal that the situation is more informal and relaxed. These variations also are related to factors such as age, gender, education, socioeconomic status, and personality.

We call this type of shift a change in language register; that is, how language is used in a particular setting or for a particular purpose. People change their speech register depending on such sociolinguistic variables as

- formality of situation;
- attitude toward topic;
- attitude toward listeners; and
- relation of speaker to others.

Changing speech registers may be completely subconscious for native speakers. For example, if a university professor takes her car in for servicing, the manner and speech she uses to communicate with the mechanic significantly differs from the manner and speech she uses to deliver a lecture. If she were to use a formal tone and academic vocabulary, the mechanic might think the professor was being condescending or might not understand what the professor was saying. Likewise, when the mechanic explains the mechanical diagnosis, the mechanic most likely chooses a simplified vocabulary rather than technical language, or jargon, which the professor wouldn't understand. Using the jargon of a profession or field with which the listener is unfamiliar will likely make the listener feel stupid or inferior and perhaps make him or her think that the speaker is inconsiderate.

Social Language

Language registers also are used deliberately to establish a social identity. Hispanics deliberately refer to themselves as La Raza (the race) to imply dignity and pride for who they are and where they come from. Using a Spanish term when speaking English is called **code switching**. This term has become a part of the American vocabulary. Symbolically it represents both the Hispanics' distinction and their integration into American culture.

ESOL teachers should be aware of these sociolinguistic functions of language and compare different social functions of language for their students. Knowing and being able to use appropriate registers allows learners to function more effectively in social situations. Learners must acquire both the social and linguistic aspects of American English. Sociolinguistic functions of a language are best acquired by using the language in authentic situations.

Sociolinguistic diversity, language variations based on regional and social differences, affects teachers' language, attitudes, and practices. Teachers must respect the validity of any group or individual's language patterns while teaching traditional English. Vernacular versions of English have well-established patterns and rules to support them. Making learners aware of language variations leads to increased interest in language learning and better ability to switch among one or more registers or dialects and Standard English.

ELLs tend to adapt linguistic structures to their familiar culture, modifying specific concepts and practices. Teachers must identify these variations, call attention to them, and teach the appropriate English equivalent. The goal is not to eliminate linguistic diversity but rather to enable learners to control their language use so that they can use Standard English in addition to their cultural variation.

Various functional adaptations of English have great significance to the cultural groups that use them. Attempting to eliminate variations not only is futile but also creates hostility and reluctance to learn English. Stable, socially shared structures emerge from the summed effects of many individual communication practices. Firmly ingrained language patterns serve a purpose within the community that uses them. Unique variations can arise in a school venue. New, nonstandard English words can represent a particular group's identity or function as a means to solidify social relationships. As long as students recognize that a variation should not be used as if it were Standard English, there should be no problem with its use.

Academic Discourse

Academic discourse refers to formal academic learning. This includes all four language skills: listening, reading, speaking, and writing. Academic learning is important for students to succeed in school. Cummins differentiated between two types of language proficiency: BICS and CALP (see Skill 2.7). An average student can acquire BICS within two to five years of language learning, whereas CALP can take from four to seven years. Many factors are involved in the acquisition of CALP, such as age, language proficiency level, and literacy in the first language.

Explicit instruction of some key language skills—vocabulary, grammar, and genre—should be provided to students to help them learn the academic discourse necessary to succeed in a school setting.

Academic discourse includes knowledge of content-area vocabulary and the various skills and strategies that are essential to successfully complete academic tasks in a mainstream classroom. Some of these skills and strategies are inferring, classifying, analyzing, synthesizing, and evaluating. As students reach higher grades, they are required to think critically and apply this knowledge to solve problems.

With respect to reading and writing, complex grammatical structures frequently are found in academic discourse, which makes it challenging for ELLs. In addition, science and other subject-area textbooks normally use passive voice. Similarly, the use of reference, pronouns, modals, and so on is a common feature of academic discourse that might cause problems for ELLs. All the language features of academic discourse help convey the intended meaning of the author; therefore, it is necessary to explicitly teach them for students to become skilled readers and writers.

Genre is an important aspect of academic discourse. Each genre employs a unique style of writing. The organization of a text differs according to the purpose of the text—for example, mystery versus romance. Likewise, in academic reading, students come across multiple texts that vary in organization and style according to the purpose of the author and the intended audience. Students need to understand the different features of multiple texts to become efficient readers. With respect to writing, students need to determine the purpose of their writing (e.g., argumentative writing versus story writing).

Skill 2.9   **Identify phonological, morphological, semantic, pragmatic, syntactic, and discourse differences between English and other languages**

Schumm (2006) emphasizes that both the reading level characteristics and the differences between L1 and L2 are important because these may influence the assumed level of the student. Some of the questions she proposes to elicit these similarities and differences are for further evaluation of reading level characteristics:

- Is the L1 writing system logographic like Arabic, syllabic like Cherokee, or alphabetic like English and Greek?
- How does the L1 syntax compare with the L2 syntax?
- Are the spelling patterns phonetic with consistent grapheme-phoneme relationships (e.g., Spanish or French) or are there multiple vowel sounds (e.g., English)?
- Do students read from left to right and top to bottom in their L1?
- Are there true cognates (Spanish *instrucción* and English *instruction*) and false cognates (Spanish *librería* <bookstore> and English *library*) that will help or confuse the ELL?
- Are the discourse patterns and writing styles of L1 and L2 similar or different?
- Are questions with known answers asked (teacher questions) or are rhetorical questions asked?
- Is L1 writing style circular, with long sentences and many details (e.g., Spanish) or linear, with the minimum number of facts or supporting details needed to support the main idea (e.g., English)?

COMPETENCY 3.0   **Knowledge of language acquisition and development**

Skill 3.1   **Identify the major theories of first and second language acquisition that inform classroom practices**

Between ages two and three, most children will be able to use language to influence the people closest to them. Research shows that, in general, boys acquire language more slowly than girls, which means we need to consider very carefully how we involve boys in activities designed to promote early language and literacy.

Various theories, some of which are examined below, have tried to explain the **language acquisition process.**

Chomsky: Language Acquisition Device

Chomsky's theory, described as nativist, asserts that humans are born with a special biological brain mechanism, called a Language Acquisition Device (LAD). His theory supposes that the ability to learn language is innate, that nature is more important than nurture, and that experience using language is necessary only to activate the LAD. Chomsky based his assumptions on work in linguistics. His work shows that children's language development is much more complex than taught by followers of behaviorist theory, which asserts that children learn language by being rewarded for imitating. However, this theory underestimates the influence that thought (cognition) and language have on each other's development.

Piaget: Cognitive Constructivism

Piaget's central interest was children's cognitive development. He theorized that language is one way that children represent their familiar worlds. Language is a reflection of thought; it does not contribute to the development of thinking. He believed cognitive development precedes language development.

Vygotsky: Social Constructivism and Language

Unlike Chomsky and Piaget, Vygotsky's central focus was the relationship between the development of thought and language. He was interested in the ways different languages impact a person's thinking. He suggested that what Piaget saw as young children's egocentric speech was actually private speech, the child's way of using words to think about something, which progressed from social speech to thinking in words. Vygotsky viewed language first as social communication, which gradually promotes both language itself and cognition.

Recent Theorizing: Intentionality

Some contemporary researchers and theorists criticize earlier theories and suggest that children, their behaviors, and their attempts to understand and communicate are misunderstood when the causes of language development are thought to be "outside" the child or else mechanistically "in the child's brain." They recognize that children are active learners who co-construct their worlds.

Their language development is part of their holistic development, emerging from cognitive, emotional, and social interactions. These theorists believe language development depends on the child's social and cultural environment, the people in it, and their interactions. How children represent these factors in their minds is fundamental to language development. They believe a child's agenda and the interactions the child generates promote language learning. The adult's role, actions, and speech are still important, but adults need to be able to "mind read" and adjust their side of the co-construction to relate to an individual child's understanding and interpretation.

Theories about language development help us see that enjoying "proto-conversations" with babies (treating them as people who can understand, share, and have intentions in sensitive interchanges) and truly listening to young children are the best ways to promote their language development.

Brain research has shown that the single most important factor affecting **language acquisition** is the onset of puberty. Before puberty, a person uses one area of the brain for language learning; after puberty, the person uses a different area of the brain. A person who learns a second language before reaching puberty will always process language learning as if prepubescent. A person who begins to learn a second language after the onset of puberty will likely find language learning more difficult and will depend more on repetition.

Some researchers have focused on analyzing aspects of the language to be acquired. Factors they consider include the following:

- Error analysis: recognizing patterns of errors
- Interlanguage: analyzing what aspects of the target language are universal
- Developmental patterns: the order in which features of a language are acquired and the sequence in which a specific feature is acquired.

Stephen Krashen developed a **theory of second language acquisition** that helps explain the processes adults use when learning a second language:

The Acquisition-Learning Hypothesis: There is a difference between "learning" a language and "acquiring" it. Children "acquire" a second language using the same process they used to learn their first language. However, adults who know only one language have to "learn" a language through coursework, studying, and memorizing. One can acquire a second language, but often it requires more deliberate interaction within that language.

The Monitor Hypothesis: The learned language "monitors" the acquired language. In other words, a person's "grammar check" kicks in and keeps awkward, incorrect language out of a person's L2 communication.

The Natural Order Hypothesis: Learning grammatical structures is predictable and follows a "natural order."

The Input Hypothesis: A language learner will learn best when the instruction or conversation is just above the learner's ability. That way, the learner has the foundation to understand most of the language but will have to figure out, often in context, the unknown elements. Some people call this "comprehensible input."

The Affective Filter Hypothesis: People will learn a second language when they are relaxed, have a high level of motivation, and have a decent level of self-confidence.

Skill 3.2   **Identify and compare first and second language acquisition processes that affect student learning**

Teaching students who are learning English as a second language poses some unique challenges, particularly in a standards-based environment. Teachers should teach with the student's developmental level in mind. Instruction should not be "dummied-down" for ESOL students. Teachers should use different approaches to ensure that these students get multiple opportunities to learn and practice English while learning content.

L1 and L2 learning follow many, if not all, of the same steps:

- **Silent Period:** The learner knows perhaps 500 receptive words but feels uncomfortable producing speech. The absence of speech does not indicate a lack of learning, and teachers should not try to force the learner to speak. Teachers can check comprehension by having the learner point or mime. This is also known as the Receptive or Preproduction stage.

- **Private Speech:** The learner knows about 1,000 receptive words and speaks in one- or two-word phrases. The learner can use simple responses, such as yes/no and either/or. This is also known as the Early Production stage.

- **Lexical Chunks:** The learner knows about 3,000 receptive words and can communicate using short phrases and sentences. Long sentences typically have grammatical errors. This is also known as the Speech Emergence stage.

- **Formulaic Speech:** The learner knows about 6,000 receptive words and begins to make complex statements, state opinions, ask for clarification, share thoughts, and speak at greater length. This is also known as the Intermediate Language Proficiency stage.

- **Experimental or Simplified Speech:** The learner develops a level of fluency and can make semantic and grammar generalizations. This is also known as the Advanced Language Proficiency stage.

Researchers disagree on whether the development of Formulaic Speech and Experimental or Simplified Speech is the same for L1 and L2 learners. Regardless, understanding that students must go through a predictable, sequential series of stages helps teachers recognize the student's progress and respond effectively. Providing comprehensible input will help students advance their language learning at any stage.

Skill 3.3   **Use research-based models of instruction including bilingual, sheltered, and/or inclusion**

The major models of ESOL programs differ depending on the sources consulted. However, general consensus recognizes the following program models with different instructional methods used in the different programs.

Immersion Education Models

With these programs, instruction is initiated in the student's non-native language, using the second language as the medium of instruction for both academic content and the second language. Two of these models strive for full bilingualism: one is for language-majority students and the other is for language minorities.

- **English Language Development (ELD) or English as a Second Language (ESL) Pull-out:** Pull-out programs include various approaches to teaching English to non-native speakers. In 1997, TESOL standards defined these approaches as marked by an intent to teach the ELL to communicate in social settings, engage in academic tasks, and use English in socially and culturally appropriate ways. The following are three well-known approaches to ELD or ESL:

    o **Grammar-based ESL:** This method teaches about the language, stressing its structure, functions, and vocabulary through rules, drills, and error correction. Widdowson (1978) refers to this type of instruction or knowledge of the language as **usage**.
    o **Communication-based ESL:** This approach emphasizes instruction in English that emphasizes *using* the language in meaningful contexts. There is little stress on correctness in the early stages and more emphasis on comprehensible input to foster communication and lower anxiety when taking risks. Widdowson (1978) refers to this type of language knowledge as **use**.
    o **Content-based ESL:** Instruction in English that attempts to develop language skills and prepare ELLs to study grade-level content material in English is content-based. There is emphasis on language, but with graded introduction to content areas, vocabulary, and basic concepts.

- **Structured English immersion:** The goal is English proficiency. ELLs are pulled out for structured instruction in English so that subject matter is comprehensible. This approach is used with sizeable groups of ELLs who speak the same language and are in the same grade level or with diverse populations of language-minority students. There is little or no L1 language support. Teachers use sheltered instructional techniques and have strong receptive skills in the students' native or heritage language.

- **Submersion with primary language support:** The goal is English proficiency. Bilingual teachers or aides support the minority students in each grade level who are ELLs. In small groups, the ELLs are tutored by reviewing the content areas in their primary language. The teachers use the L1 to support English content classes; ELLs achieve limited literacy in L1.

- **Canadian French immersion (language-majority students):** The goal is bilingualism in French (L2) and English (L1). The targeted population is the language majority. Students are immersed in the L2 for the first two years using sheltered language instruction, and then the L1 is introduced. The goal is all students of the majority language (English) becoming fluent in L2 (French).

- **Indigenous language immersion (endangered languages, such as Navajo):** The goal is bilingualism. The program is socially, linguistically, and cognitively attuned to the native culture and community context. This approach supports endangered minority languages and develops academic skills in minority language and culture and in the English language and predominate culture.

Push-In Model

In the push-in model, the ESL teacher goes into the classroom to assist ELLs. ESL teachers need to establish good working relationships with the regular classroom teacher and establish the kind of collaboration they will have with the regular teacher to co-teach the ELLs. Fulton-Scott and Calvin (1983) suggest that students achieve more benefits from this method because of the interaction with English-proficient speakers.

Sheltered Instruction

Sheltered instruction (Specially Designed Academic Instruction in English—SDAIE) is an approach in ESOL teaching that integrates the classroom content with English language instruction. The approach tries to provide mainstream, grade-level content (social studies, math, and science) instruction and promote development of English language proficiency at the same time.

Inclusion

Inclusion is the educational practice of placing children with disabilities in the classroom with children without disabilities. This educational model is a result of PL 94-142, the Education of All Handicapped Children Act of 1975. The law is based upon the principles of the Equal Protection Clause of the Fourteenth Amendment. Free and Appropriate Public Education (FAPE) and Least Restrictive Environment (LRE) are two important concepts resulting from the law.

Different states and school districts have interpreted the law differently, but increasingly special education students are included in the mainstream classroom for all or part of the day.

The following are the two main models:

- Push in: The special education teacher works with the special needs student in a supporting role to the mainstream teacher.
- Full inclusion: The special education teacher is a full partner in the mainstream classroom. Even though the child has an IEP, the general teacher is responsible for its implementation.

Teachers who work with special needs students frequently use **differentiation** to enable these students to achieve full academic success. Differentiation involves providing a range of activities and using a variety of strategies for children with different abilities, from learning disabled to gifted, to learn successfully in the same classroom. Although ELLs are not classified as leaning disabled, some of them may be.

Skill 3.4   **Determine characteristics of bilingualism**

Bilingualism is a process that occurs over time. It requires commitment, encouragement, and language routines. Exposing a child to more than one language from birth initially may delay speech, but it will allow the child to become equally fluent in both languages. All four manifestations of language use (speaking, hearing, writing, and reading) should be encouraged and practiced.

Bilingual learners frequently speak at least one language with an accent, the pronunciation characteristics of a particular group. Accents may be reduced or disappear entirely over time, but they sometimes require specific accent reduction study. Fluency, or the speed with which a learner can correctly speak the language, normally increases with time and practice. Individual learning progression varies profoundly among learners. Teachers always must be prepared to provide comprehensible input based on the individual level of each student. In addition, teachers must be alert to interference that occurs between the two languages.

Skill 3.5   **Determine the factors that influence the development of bilingualism**

A number of factors influence bilingualism. A learner's reason for learning a second language can provide significant motivation or can inhibit language learning. The level of immersion greatly affects progress. Many language teachers dislike the block schedule because learners only use the second language every other day. Social attitudes also affect learning. Some communities greatly value second language learning, while others consider it insignificant or a cultural threat.

The family and home environment greatly affects bilingualism. In homes where only the first language is spoken, the learner has no opportunity to practice the second language with family members. When family members speak both languages, they can choose from a number of strategies for encouraging bilingualism, including having one parent speak to the learner exclusively in the L1 and the other in the L2; having both parents divide their speaking time between the two languages; determining what is the most useful division of speaking time between the L1 and the L2; or allowing second language learning to take place entirely outside the home. When possible, most experts recommend using both languages with the child as early as possible.

Learners use **cognitive processes** to organize and direct second language acquisition. Examples of these processes are methods of approaching the learning of new information and choices regarding what to ignore and what to pay attention to (Díaz-Rico and Weed 1995). Developing these skills leads to language acquisition, but these skills also bridge languages and enhance cognitive skills in the first language.

Research shows that learning and using more than one language

- enhances problem-solving and analytical skills;
- allows better formation of concepts;
- increases visual-social abilities;
- furthers logical reasoning; and
- supports cognitive flexibility.

Cognitive skills are any mental skills that are used in the process of acquiring knowledge, including reasoning, perception, and intuition. Using these skills in second language learning applies L2 vocabulary and sentence patterns to thought processes that already have formed in the L1.

Memorizing the words and rules of a second language is insufficient to integrate the second language in the learner's thought patterns. L2 learners use cognitive processes to form rules, which allow them to understand and create novel utterances. The creation of novel utterances, whether grammatically correct or not, offers proof that the L2 learner is not just mimicking chunks of prescribed language but rather is using cognitive processes to acquire the second language. People use their own thinking processes, or cognition, to discover the rules of the language they are acquiring.

See also Skill 3.8.

Skill 3.6   Identify how ELLs' use of home language serves as a foundation for learning English

Language, barring physical disabilities or isolation from other humans, is universal. Developing language is a lifelong process in one's native language, and one goes through similar processes to thoroughly acquire or learn a foreign language.

Many studies have found that cognitive and academic development in the **first language** has an extremely important and positive effect on second language schooling (e.g., Bialystok 1991; Collier 1989, 1992; Garcia 1994; Genesee 1987, 1994; Thomas and Collier 1995). It therefore is important that language learners continue to develop their first language skills because the most gifted five year old is approximately halfway through the process of first language development. From ages 6 to 12, the child continues to acquire subtle phonological distinctions, vocabulary, semantics, syntax, formal discourse patterns, and the complexities of pragmatics in the oral system of his or her first language (Berko Gleason 1993).

These skills can be transferred to acquiring or learning a second language. When ELLs already know how to read and write in their first language (L1), they can transfer many of their primary language skills to their target language. They already have learned the relationship between print and spoken language. That print can be used for many different things and that writing conveys messages from its author. Grellet (1981) has stated that the knowledge "one brings to the text is often more important than what one finds in it." Teachers can build on this previous knowledge and address specifics in English as they arise.

Skill 3.7   Determine factors that affect ELLs' learning of English, including psychological, social, cultural, and political factors

Acculturation is the process of becoming accustomed to the customs, language, practices, and environment of a new culture. The factors that influence this process include, but are not limited to, the learner's desire and ability to become a part of the dominant culture.

In a study of students' school performance, Ogbu (1978) creates divisions among groups of immigrants. Minority groups categorized as "caste-like minorities" include groups that were integrated into a society that they did not choose and in which they were exploited, typically through slavery. Such minorities typically work minimum-wage and undesirable jobs and are unable to move beyond their current situation, regardless of their language skills. Because of this social and economic enslavement, academic achievement is seldom important or a goal and assimilation into the culture is limited to a low-status position. In contrast, groups (such as recent immigrants from Central and South America, Eastern Europe, and Asia) described as "immigrant minorities," which have not suffered the same social stigma, recognize education as a tool for advancement and place a much higher value on it. ELLs in this group have a strong incentive for learning English and adapting to the culture around them.

The relationship between acquiring a second language and adopting the new culture is strong. Schumann (1978a) has developed a model of acculturation that asserts, "the degree to which a learner acculturates to the target language group will control the degree to which he acquires the second language" (34). Or, put another way, "the level to which a learner can assimilate into the culture will dictate the level of second language proficiency." According to his model, the following social elements impact the acculturation process:

- The primary (L1) and English language groups (L2) view each other with mutual respect, have optimistic attitudes, and are compatible.
- The L1 and L2 groups both wish for the primary group to assimilate into the culture.
- The L1 and L2 groups agree/accept to share social services and conveniences.
- The L1 group wants to remain in the area beyond a temporary status.

These factors assist in the L1 group's process of acquiring English, which facilitates acceptance. Likewise, the absence of these factors can contribute to the L1 group not learning English and remaining outside the dominant culture. In a classroom setting, if there is no mutual respect, positive attitude, or sense of compatibility between the L1 and L2 groups, successful second language acquisition for the L1 group is severely hindered. In turn, without a common language, the chances of acceptance and assimilation become significantly reduced.

Classroom and school activities that promote interactions among ELLs and native speakers encourage language growth and an exchange of cultures. With an increased ability to communicate, learners discover commonalities and form friendships. Sports, music, art, photography, and other school activities that allow ELLs to participate while they learn more language are excellent opportunities for increasing acculturation.

Schools that find innovative ways to attract families to participate in the school have greater success in gaining parental support for academic goals. Providing translators at school meetings is one way to include non-English speaking family members and make them feel welcome and a part of the school's culture. When ELL families participate in the school, cultural barriers diminish and student academic performance improves.

See also Skill 3.5.

Skill 3.8   **Apply individual learner variables to guide the process of learning English as a Second Language**

The term *affective domain* refers to the range of feelings and emotions that affects how a second language is acquired. Self-esteem, motivation, anxiety, and attitude all contribute to the second language acquisition process. Internal and external factors influence the affective domain. ESOL teachers must be aware of each student's personality and must stay especially attuned to the affective factors in their students.

Self-esteem: Learning a second language puts learners in a vulnerable frame of mind. While some learners are less inhibited about taking risks, all learners can be shut down if their comfort level is surpassed. Using teaching techniques that lower stress and emphasize group participation rather than focusing on individuals getting the right answer reduces anxiety and encourages learners to attempt to use the new language.

Motivation: Researchers Gardner and Lambert (1972) have identified two types of motivation for learning a second language:

- **Instrumental motivation:** acquiring a second language for a specific reason, such as a job
- **Integrative motivation:** acquiring a second language to fulfill a wish to communicate within a different culture

Neither type of motivation stands alone. Instructors recognize that motivation can be viewed as either a "trait" or a "state." As a trait, motivation is more permanent and culturally acquired; as a state, motivation is considered temporary because it fluctuates depending on rewards and penalties.

Anxiety: Anxiety is inherent in second language learning. Students are required to take risks, such as speaking in front of their peers. Without a native's grasp of the language, second language learners are unable to express their individuality, which is even more threatening and uncomfortable. However, not all anxiety is debilitative. Bailey's (1983) research demonstrates that facilitative anxiety (anxiety that compels an individual to stay on task) is a positive factor for some learners, closely related to competitiveness.

Attitude: Attitude typically evolves from internalized feelings about oneself and one's ability to learn a language. However, one's attitude about language and the speakers of that language is largely external and influenced by the surrounding environment of classmates and family.

If non-native speakers of English experience discrimination because of their accent or cultural status, their attitude toward the value of second language learning may diminish. Schools can significantly improve the attitude toward SLAs (second language acquisition) by encouraging activities between native speakers and ELLs. This can be beneficial to both groups if students learning the SLA's first language work on projects together. When native speakers get a chance to appreciate the SLA's language skill in their first language, attitudes change and ELLs have an opportunity to shine.

In some cultures, children who learn a second language at the expense of their primary language might be viewed as "turncoats" by family and friends. This can cause negative feelings about school in general and can adversely affect second language acquisition.

Skill 3.9   **Distinguish characteristics of social language (e.g., basic interpersonal communication skills [BICS]) and academic language (e.g., cognitive academic language proficiency [CALP])**

Language skills used to communicate with others in everyday activities are called in **basic interpersonal communication skills (BICS).** Children acquire BICS naturally in their social environment from their parents, teachers, other children, and the media. Gestures, body language, and facial expressions offer contextual support to learners as they try to acquire these skills. Acquiring BICS generally takes from six months to two years (Cummins 1999–2003) after first being exposed to a second language.

From their earliest days in a school system, children are molded by BICS. They must learn to ask for permission to go to the bathroom; ask for their food in the cafeteria; state their name, address, and telephone number; explain who their parents are and what they do; ask for help in tying their shoes; state if they are cold or hot and feeling well or feel sick; learn to use their "inside" voice versus their "outside" voice in the classroom; and so forth.

Instructors help ELLs by modeling the correct language, requiring students to raise their hand to ask for permission, supplying the correct item when it is requested, motivating the students with stickers or stamps on their hands, and congratulating the students when they learn a new BICS.

Cognitive academic language proficiency (CALP) refers to the language skills required for academic achievement and usually is more difficult to acquire than BICS. Cummins (1993–2003) states that it takes from five to seven years for students to acquire CALP after initial exposure to a second language.

The following list demonstrates Cummins' four levels of difficulty:

- **Level 1: Cognitive undemanding / context-embedded**
  Examples: talking with friends; ordering book in the library; playing sports; talking at parties

- **Level 2: Cognitively undemanding / context-reduced**
  Ordering book by phone; following instructions from a recorded message; reading a letter from a pen pal

- **Level 3: Cognitively demanding / context-embedded**
  Solving a math problem using graphs, charts, etc.; doing a hands-on science experiment; playing an interactive computer game

- **Level 4: Cognitive demanding / Context-reduced**
  Proving math theorems; writing a research report; listening to a lecture on an unfamiliar subject

Academic tasks tend to increase in their cognitive demands as students progress in their schooling, but the context becomes increasingly reduced. ELLs who have not developed CALP need additional teacher support to achieve success.

Contextual support in the form of realia, demonstrations, pictures, graphs, and so on provide the ELL with scaffolding and reduce the language difficulty level of the task.

Skill 3.10　　Identify sources of ELLs' errors (e.g., interlanguage) to guide effective instruction

Interlanguage is a strategy a second language learner uses to compensate for his or her lack of proficiency while learning a second language. It can be classified as neither L1 nor L2—rather, it could almost be considered an L3, complete with its own grammar and lexicon. The learner develops interlanguage in relation to his or her experiences (both positive and negative) with the second language. Larry Selinker introduced the theory of interlanguage in 1972 and asserted that L2 learners create certain learning strategies to compensate in the in-between period while they acquire the language. The following are some of the learning strategies that the learner may use:

- Overgeneralization
- Simplification
- L1 interference or language transfer

These practices create an interlanguage, which assists the learner in moving from one stage to the next during second language acquisition. For example, **L1 interference or language transfer** occurs when a learner's primary language influences his or her progress in the L2. Interference most commonly affects pronunciation, grammar structures, vocabulary, and semantics.

Overgeneralization occurs when the learner attempts to apply a rule across the board, without regard to exceptions. **Simplification** occurs when the L2 learner uses resources that require limited vocabulary to aid comprehension and allow the learner to listen, read, and speak in the target language at a very elementary level.

Selinker theorizes that a psychological structure is "awakened" when a learner begins the process of second language acquisition. He attaches great significance to the notion that the learner and the native speaker would not create similar sounds if they attempted to communicate the same thought, idea, or meaning. **Fossilization** is a term Selinker applies to the process in which an L1 learner reaches a plateau and accepts that less-than-fluent level, which prevents the learner from achieving L2 fluency. Fossilization occurs when non-L1 forms become fixed in the interlanguage of the L2 learner. L2 learners are highly susceptible to this phenomenon during the early stages.

S. P. Corder is most noted for his work in **error analysis**, a field that until 1970 was not fully recognized (Ellis 1994). Corder drew a line, separating errors of skill (or competency) from errors in presentation (or performance). During the 1970s, when researchers were searching for reasons behind errors of skill/competencies, J. Richards conducted a study in which he found the following reasons for learner errors:

- **L1 transfers:** L1 transfer or L1 interference occurs when a learner's L1 influences his or her progress in L2. Pronunciation, grammar structures, vocabulary, and semantics commonly are affected.

- **Overgeneralization:** Overgeneralization occurs when the learner attempts to apply a grammatical rule to instances in which it does not apply. A learner is overgeneralizing when he or she applies a grammatical rule to all verbs and does not account for exceptions. For example, a learner is overgeneralizing when he or she attempts to apply *-ed* to create a past tense of an irregular verb, such as "buyed" or "swimmed."

- **Simplification:** Simplification is the practice of modifying language to facilitate comprehension. Researchers disagree on the value of this practice. Krashen believes that simplification aids L2 acquisition. Others believe that lessening authentic texts diminishes L2 learners' ability to comprehend more difficult texts.

Research shows that correcting semantic errors ("No, that's not a house, it's a skyscraper") contributes to language learning. However, correcting every grammatical error creates a negative atmosphere that makes students afraid to express themselves for fear of making a mistake and being corrected. Students also lose fluency if they try to analyze rules and grammar before speaking.

The problem of identifying learners' misconceptions hinges on making a correct analysis and diagnosis of the learners' input. Teachers often misinterpret the intended meaning of a learner's speech. Teachers may believe that if they are familiar with students and their first language, they are more likely to guess a learner's intended meaning. This approach assumes that errors in English differ according to the learner's first language and that understanding common types of errors typical of a particular first language can help a teacher approach student errors more effectively and provide focused practice. For example, Spanish speakers often pronounce the consonant "s" as "es" because many Spanish words begin this way. Because the word for "study" in Spanish is "estudiar," many Spanish-speaking ELLs pronounce words such as "student" as "estudent." A teacher can cluster these words and create ways to practice this type of word.

An alternative, cognitive approach uses general knowledge that can apply to a variety of languages. This approach uses a unifying linguistic theory that encompasses all human languages in a universal framework. It describes languages as a set of interlocking principles and introduces parameters to account for the variations among languages. In this approach, the diagnoses are made following patterns of acquisition that this theory defines, mirroring the language acquisition process.

Research has shown the traditional practice of correcting written work by providing a corrected version of writing to be ineffective. Students cannot integrate large numbers of corrections into their cognitive processes, and visually, a page with as much teacher writing as student writing demoralizes a student who has made a concerted effort to express ideas. A better approach is to note one example each of up to three types of error and explain proper usage to the individual or to the class if many learners make the same type of error.

Skill 3.11   **Identify language functions (e.g., communicating needs, purpose, desires) of spoken and written English to facilitate English language acquisition**

Functions are things you can do with English, such as communicating needs (I need to go to the bathroom), purpose (I did my homework early so I could go to the mall), desires (I want to finish school and go on to college); making requests (Could I see your paper, please?); making offers (Everyone who finishes their work in the next two minutes can play a board game); and apologizing (I am sorry. I didn't mean to upset you). Purely functional English is rare; we usually incorporate notions into our speech and writing.

Notions (Wilkins 1976) are concepts that language expresses. Concepts include existence, motion, number, time, place, color, and so on. They generally look like typical vocabulary items such as *man*, *evening*, and *bright blue sky*.

COMPETENCY 4.0   **Knowledge of second language literacy development**

Skill 4.1   **Determine and apply current theories of second language reading development for ELLs at varying English proficiency levels**

Children learn to read only once. If they are able to read in their native language, they are able to read in English. It is important for ELLs to increase their vocabulary and knowledge of the structure of English, their second language. By building on what the ELL already knows with regards to literacy, language, and experiences in his or her native language, teachers are able to improve the reading level of the ELL in English. For this reason, it is necessary to evaluate the ELL in his or her first, native, or heritage language to initiate the best reading instruction in English.

Chall (1983) was the first to study reading stages. She proposed six stages of reading that change over time as children progress through school:

- 0 Prereading: typical of preschool through late kindergarten (also called pre-alphabetic, logographic, pre-conventional)
- 1 Initial reading or alphabetic decoding: typical of kindergarten through early second grade (also called alphabetic decoding stage)
- 2 Confirmation and fluency: typical of second and third grades
- 3 Reading to learn: typical of fourth through eighth grades
- 4 Multiple points of view: typical of high school
- 5 Construction and reconstruction: typical of college and adulthood

Later studies have modified Chall's work. Newer studies emphasize the integration of processing skills and the importance of sound, spelling, and meaning in learning words. These elements develop together on a continuum. Rich text environments are crucial to the growth process.

Ehri (1996) developed a continuum of word reading development that demonstrated how children master the alphabetic principle. Children cannot retain more than a few dozen sight words, and they only progress if they are able to relate letters to sounds. For many ELLs, this is particularly difficult if their language is phonetic because English is not. English has roughly 44 sounds corresponding to 26 letters, while Spanish, for example, has direct letter-sound correspondence. For phonetic readers, decoding English words can be difficult.

- The Logographic Phase: Child may
  - try to remember words by incidental visual characteristics;
  - treat words as pictograms and make a direct association to meaning; and
  - equate the length of the word with its meaning.

- The Novice Alphabetic Phase: Child may
  - identify first consonant in word, must learn to separate all sounds;
  - rely on letter names to identify word, needs to distinguish between letter sounds and their names; and
  - confuse similar words, needs to decode the whole word, left to right, with sound-symbol links.

- The Mature Alphabetic Phase: Child
    - can sound out regular one-syllable words;
    - can increase speed of whole word recognition when decoding becomes accurate;
    - has well-established phonemic awareness;
    - can represent almost every sound with a logical letter choice; and
    - can represent and recognize spelling patterns, words of more than one syllable, meaningful parts of words, and basic sight vocabulary.

- The Orthographic Phase: Child can
    - read words using phonemes, syllabic units, morpheme units, and whole words;
    - use sequential and hierarchical decoding (i.e., notices familiar parts first, then decodes unfamiliar parts);
    - remember multisyllabic words; and
    - use knowledge of word origin, syntactic role, ending rules, prefix, suffix, and root forms to decode words and their meanings.

Research shows that students who are proficient readers in L1 have more reading success in L2 (Collier and Thomas 1989; Ovando et al. 2003; Snow, Burns, and Griffin 1998). This prompts the question, "What role does the oral second language play in the reading process?" In general, bilingual education models maintain the idea that ELLs be at least at the level of speech emergence before reading instruction begins. However, given the increasing variation in the U.S. school population, many believe that it is no longer equitable to wait for oral proficiency before beginning reading instruction. Anderson and Roit (1998) argue that reading instruction should be used with certain L2 learners and avoided with others. When instruction is well planned and teachers consider the individual students' needs, all ELLs can benefit from reading instruction in L2.

Skill 4.2   **Determine and apply current theories of second language writing development for ELLs at varying English proficiency levels**

Just like native English speakers, ELL students have to manage many different skills to become proficient writers, including clarity of thought and expression, how to use different genres to convey different purposes in writing, and conventional spelling, grammar, and punctuation. Since these skills vary for each specific type of writing, it is difficult to discuss writing stages. Even so, it is important for teachers to have a general guide on which to base their instruction plans.

The following chart, based on a writing matrix developed by Peregoy and Boyle (2008), offers a good guide to identifying characteristics of a student's writing level. It encompasses three developmental levels and six traits.

- Trait 1: Fluency
Beginning Level: Writes one or two short sentences.
Intermediate Level: Writes several sentences.
Advanced Level: Writes a paragraph or more.

- Trait 2: Organization
  Beginning Level: Lacks logical sequence or is so short that organization presents no problem.
  Intermediate Level: Somewhat sequenced.
  Advanced Level: Follows standard organization for genre.

- Trait 3: Grammar
  Beginning Level: Basic word-order problems. Uses only present-tense form.
  Intermediate Level: Minor grammatical errors.
  Advanced Level: Grammar resembles that of native speaker of same age.

- Trait 4: Vocabulary
  Beginning Level: Limited vocabulary. Needs to rely at times on L1 or ask for translation.
  Intermediate Level: Knows most words needed to express ideas but lacks vocabulary for finer shades of meaning.
  Advanced Level: Flexible in word choice; similar to good native writer of same age.

- Trait 5: Genre
  Beginning Level: Does not differentiate form to suit purpose.
  Intermediate Level: Chooses form to suit purpose but limited in choices of expository forms.
  Advanced Level: Knows several genres; makes appropriate choices. Similar to effective native writers of same age.

- Trait 6: Sentence variety
  Beginning Level: Uses one or two sentence patterns.
  Intermediate Level: Uses several sentence patterns.
  Advanced Level: Uses a good variety of sentence patterns effectively.

Skill 4.3   Identify how ELLs' L1 oral language influences the use of oral and written English in the classroom

ELLs' L1 oral language has a tremendous influence on their performance in the ESL classroom. Many children have difficulty pronouncing English when they arrive in the English language classroom. They may have been introduced to English in their country or home, but they do not speak it fluently. Most probably will not have read in English extensively and will not be familiar with writing in English. (If they are familiar with text messaging, this is not Standard English and will have to be ignored for most classroom work.)

According to Krashen, all language learners undergo the same steps to arrive at a language:

MORPHEME ACQUISITION ORDER in SECOND LANGUAGE ACQUISITION

Stage 1	-ing, plural, copula
Stage 2	auxiliary verb, article
Stage 3	irregular past tense verbs
Stage 4	regular past tense verbs, third-person singular, possessives

(After Krashen 1977)

ELLs seem to know that speaking is one of the most important language skills to acquire. Often they are hesitant to speak because of inhibitions, having nothing to say, low or uneven participation among the different speakers, and frequent use of the mother tongue with peers (Ur 1996). Yet, teachers must encourage ELLs to use English as much as possible because in learning to express themselves orally, ELLs are better equipped to perform other language tasks such as listening, reading, and writing.

See also Skill 3.10.

Skill 4.4   **Identify how ELLs' home literacy practices (e.g., oral, written) influence the development of oral and written English**

Although literacy varies among families, it serves many functions in families living below the poverty level, families in which English is not the primary language, and families with low educational levels (Peregoy and Boyle 2008). Teachers need to be perceptive and draw upon the child's home language and literacy experiences to best serve the child when beginning literacy instruction.

Encouraging home involvement in the literacy process is critical. Family members model reading and writing every time they read the newspaper or a magazine, make a shopping list, note an appointment on a calendar, discuss their work schedule, or discuss charges on the most recent phone bill. Many children come from societies in which oral storytelling traditions (e.g., Navajo, Spanish, Hmong, or African American) provide excellent foundations for literacy development.

Nevertheless, little research has been conducted about how to teach English to ELLs, regardless of age, who have limited literacy in their first language. If feasible, students should learn to read first in their native language and later the second language. When instruction is begun in English, many ESOL practitioners believe that the same methods used to teach the native speaker will be beneficial to the ELL because similar literacy patterns will probably emerge. Older learners may be able to progress more rapidly because they use their experiences to help them with comprehension and communication.

National reading authorities recommend phonemic awareness, phonics, reading fluency, and comprehension as the keys to achieving literacy. All of these elements should be considered meaningful in context rather than in isolation. Instruction in specific strategies (e. g., summarizing, retelling, answering questions) will help ELLs become independent readers and writers.

Skill 4.5   **Select methods to incorporate students' L1 literacy into English language literacy development (e.g., transfer)**

Peregoy and Boyle (2008) state that literacy scaffolding helps ELLs with reading and writing at a level that otherwise would be impossible for them. Scaffolding allows ELLs to work at their level in both reading and writing and, at the same time, challenges them to reach their next level of development. To help students achieve their level, several criteria are suggested:

- Use of functional, meaningful communication found in whole texts
- Use of language and discourse patterns that repeat themselves and are predictable
- A model (from teacher or peers) for understanding and producing particular written language patterns
- Support of students at a level Krashen describes as $i + 1$
- Discarding supports when the student no longer needs them

Keeping in mind the scaffolding theory, teachers may use the first language in instruction—when they know it. This is not always possible. In many states, there are hundreds of language communities represented in the statewide school system. A danger of this method is that some students become dependent on instruction in their first language and are reluctant to utilize their knowledge of the second language. However, for most children, instruction in their first language has numerous advantages. First, language instruction lowers the affective filter by reducing tension, anxiety, and even fear, thus permitting faster learning. Second, it can clarify misunderstandings in the second language content. Finally, it can be used to explain how the two languages differ or are the same with respect to different types of reading texts or writing tasks.

Schemata needs to be activated to draw upon the ELL's previous knowledge and learning, especially when the ELL may not have had experiences similar to those of learners in the mainstream culture. The use of graphics (e.g., brainstorming, web maps, and organizational charts) to encourage pre-reading thoughts about a topic activates this knowledge and shows how information is organized in the students' minds. Schumm (2006) states that research has shown the following:

- More prior knowledge permits a reader to understand and remember more (Brown, Bransford, Ferrara, and Campione 1983).
- Prior knowledge must be activated to improve comprehension (Bransford and Johnson 1972).
- Failure to activate prior knowledge is one cause of poor readers (Paris and Lindauer 1976).
- Good readers accept new information if they are convinced by an author's arguments. Likewise, they may reject ideas when they conflict with a reader's prior knowledge (Pressley 2000).

COMPETENCY 5.0   **Knowledge of ESL/ESOL research, history, public policy, and current practices**

Skill 5.1   **Identify past and present approaches to ESOL instruction (e.g., grammar-translation, audio-lingual, Communicative Language Teaching, Natural Approach, TPR, CALLA, SIOP)**

Grammar-translation: This method began in Prussia at the end of the eighteenth century and was rooted in the teaching of Latin and Greek, "the languages of intellectuals". These ancient languages were used to teach modern languages. Their grammatical terminology and techniques were adapted into modern languages. Textbooks consisted of abstract grammatical rules, lists of vocabulary, and sentences for translation. The purpose of this method was to teach students to read in the foreign language and to write it accurately. Today, these techniques are still used, often in conjunction with other techniques.

Audio-lingual: Based on the work of many linguists (e.g., Fries, Bloomfield, Brooks, et. al), the U.S. Army developed an intensive method to train 100,000 personnel in 50 different languages to meet the exigencies of World War II. The methodology demanded intensive contact (10 hours per day, 6 days a week), mature and highly motivated students, specially trained instructors, and native speakers for conversation. The program was highly successful. When adapted into high schools, it was not as successful where like conditions did not exist.

Communicative Language Teaching (CLT): CLT has three main characteristics: a whole-person approach, process learning, and teachers as facilitators. The learner is a responsible individual with close ties to the others in the group and is responsible for his or her learning. Emphasis is on the process of learning the language and not its end product or perfect utterances. Teachers transmit knowledge rather than "teach"; teaching is subordinate to learning.

Natural Approach: T. Terrell and S. Krashen are the researchers behind the most comprehensive CBA/CBL approach: the Natural Approach. The underlying assumption is that any learner of any age has the ability to receive comprehensible speech input and determine its pattern, without someone else having to "spell it out." According to Terrell and Krashen, the approach involves large amounts of comprehensible input, whether it is situational, from visual aids/cues, or grammatical. This input is "respectful" of "the initial preproduction period, expecting speech to emerge not from artificial practice, but from motivated language use, progressing from early single-word responses up to more and more coherent discourse" (Celce-Murcia 1991). They also maintain that being "grammatically correct" is not as important as the learner enjoying the learning process. Critics of Terrell and Krashen maintain that by not correcting the learner's errors early, the learner achieves fluency at the expense of accuracy.

Total Physical Response (TPR): TPR is a CBA-based approach developed by J. Asher in the 1960s. The main premise underlying TPR is that children begin to learn when situations require them to give a meaningful action response rather than a verbal one. The TPR approach is not as demanding or intimidating as other approaches because it allows the learner to casually acquire the basic comprehensive skills needed for future L2 proficiency (Celce-Murcia 1991).

Cognitive Academic Language Learning Approach (CALLA): This approach assists in the transition from an ESOL-driven language arts program to a "mainstream" language arts program by teaching ELLs how to handle content-area material with success (Chamot and O'Malley 1994). CALLA helps intermediate and advanced students understand and retain content-area material while they are improving their English language skills.

CALLA lessons incorporate content-area lessons based on the grade-level curriculum in science, math, social studies, and so on. The student must acquire the language functions used in the content class, such as describing, classifying, and explaining. The learning strategy instruction will be given in critical and creative thinking skills so that ELLs develop the ability to solve problems, extrapolate, make inferences, and so on.

Sheltered Instruction Observation Protocol (SIOP): The SIOP model was developed by researchers at California State University, Long Beach (Jana Echevarria and Mary Ellen Vogt) and the Center for Applied Linguistics (Deborah J. Short) under the auspices of the Center for Research on Education, Diversity & Excellence (CREDE), a national research center funded by the U.S. Department of Education from 1996 through 2003.

The SIOP Model consists of eight interrelated components:

1. Lesson Preparation
2. Building Background
3. Comprehensible Input
4. Strategies
5. Interaction
6. Practice/Application
7. Lesson Delivery
8. Review and Assessment

Teachers design and deliver lessons that address the academic and linguistic needs of ELLs using instructional strategies connected to each of the components.

Skill 5.2   **Identify major researchers and how their contributions have affected the field of second language teaching and learning**

L. Vygotsky, S. Krashen, J. Asher, V. A. Postovsky, H. Winitz, T. Terrell, and C. Gattegno are the major researchers whose theories have shaped the evolution of second language learning strategies. J. Asher, V. A. Postovsky, H. Winitz, and T. Terrell all contributed theories for Comprehension-Based Approaches (CBA) or Comprehension-Based Learning (CBL), while C. Gattegno's research was almost anti-CBA/CBL.

CBA/CBL approaches are focused on building up the learner's receptiveness for learning listening skills and some reading skills. The case for using a CBL or CBA approach is that the processes of sending and receiving information require different mental processing because speaking is much more complex than listening. Therefore, placing extreme emphasis on speaking when learning a second language is counterproductive to positive second language acquisition (Celce-Murcia 1991).

V. A. Postovsky developed a CBA/CBL-based approach known as Delayed Oral Response (DOR). The DOR model is based on listening and visualization. Postovsky created a test program for instructing Russian through problem-solving tasks and multiple-choice answers. The learner was presented with four pictures on a screen while listening to the "problem" in Russian. The learner responded by touching one of the four pictures. If he or she selected the correct picture, then the program went to the next task. If the program did not go to the next task, then the learner knew that he or she had to try again (Celce-Murcia 1991).

H. Winitz, a professor of speech science and psychology at the University of Missouri, experimented with a model called Optimal Habit Reinforcement (OHR) and created a self-instructional program of audiocassettes and an accompanying book, which is based on the principles of CBA/CBL. The self-instructional audiocassettes and book called "The Learnables" provided no feedback to the learners. The learning was self-directed; if the learner decided that he or she did not understand the script corresponding to the picture in the book, then the learner would just rewind the tape (Celce-Murcia 1991).

Caleb Gattegno pioneered Silent Way Learning (SWL). This strategy requires that the instructor, not the learners, remain quiet while trying to elicit input from the learners. The instructor may use visual aids/cues, gestures, and so on to give hints to the learners. The learning occurs when the learners attempt to speak, testing speaking skills related to meaning, form, and function. It is entirely up to the learners to decide what they will say and which level of speech they will use: "The cardinal principle the teacher must follow is phrased in four words: Subordinate teaching to learning" (Celce-Murcia 1991).

Wilkins (1976) developed a system of language learning based on "notions" (concepts such as location, frequency, time, and sequence) and "functions" (such as requests, threats, complaints, and offers) based on the system of meanings a learner would need to know to communicate. His notional/functional syllabus did not emphasize grammatical correctness, but accuracy was implicit in the structures students practiced.

Lewis (1993, 1997) proposed the idea of "chunks" of language that the learner must master to be able to communicate, thus firmly placing lexis back at the center of the language learning process. By learning fixed chunks (How do you do?) and semi-fixed chunks (According to the author/writer/editor, the main/principal/most interesting point to be seen is . . .), the ELL can greatly increase his or her language abilities.

Prabhu (1983) believes that language is acquired through meaning. The mental act of reasoning creates the conditions for learning. Tasks, which he classifies into three categories, are an effective way of achieving learning in the language classroom:

- **Information-gap activities:** Information is transferred from one person to another, one form to another, or one place to another.
- **Reasoning activities:** Implies the discovery through reasoning, inference, deduction, or a perception of patterns.
- **Opinion-gap activities:** Identification and expression of personal preferences or attitudes in response to a situation.

See also Skills 3.11 and 5.1.

Skill 5.3   **Relate current research to best practices in second language and literacy instruction**

The following language learning theories support specific instructional strategies.

Theory: If the instructional environment for L2 learners is characterized by high expectations for speaking correctly, total memorization of grammatical rules and vocabulary, and constant error correction, then the L2 learner will quickly lose motivation to continue the learning process.

Strategy: Total Physical Response (TPR): This is a "command-driven" instructional technique developed by psychologist James Asher. TPR is a useful tool in the early developmental stage of second language acquisition and for LEP students without any previous exposure to English. The main tenet of TPR is that input in the form of commands and gestures is comprehensible and also is fun for the L2 learner. Asher supports this theory with the process that young children use when acquiring their primary language. Children gradually develop both their awareness and attempts to communicate until listening comprehension skills have reached a comfortable level, and at this point they will begin to speak. Through TPR, instructors interact with students by way of commands/gestures, and the students respond with a "physical response."

TPR emphasizes listening rather than speaking. Students are encouraged to speak only when they feel ready.

Theory: For the L2 learner to begin production in the target language (TL), the following principles must be observed and implemented:

- During the silent period (when learners listen instead of speaking), the instructors must use comprehensible input corresponding to the learners' level of understanding in the TL.
- The L2 learner's attempts to speak and produce language will occur gradually.
- The class curriculum must be aligned with specific speech production skills. For example, instead of a linear-grammatical approach, instruction should be topically centered, such as non-sequential lessons on weather, things found in a house, or how to tell time.

Strategy: The Natural Approach: T. Terrell and S. Krashen are the researchers behind the most comprehensive CBA/CBL approach: the Natural Approach.

Theory: When learners are taught through content-based instruction such as mathematics, science, and social studies, they tend to achieve a much higher proficiency level in the TL than if they are instructed only in the TL through ESOL methods.

Strategy: The Cognitive Academic Language Learning Approach (CALLA) integrates the following tenets:

- The L2 learners' actual grade level in the main subject areas of mathematics, science, and social studies should be the deciding factor for content.
- The L2 learners should be exposed to and gradually acquire the specific language used when studying in the subject areas. For example: add this column of numbers, determine "x" in this algebraic problem, identify the properties of this cell.

- The L2 learners should be encouraged to use higher-level cognitive processes, such as application, analysis, and synthesis.

See also Skill 5.1.

Skill 5.4   Evaluate appropriate research-based models of instruction for ELLs

There is no one method or strategy that is effective in all situations or with all ELLs. Thinking today suggests an eclectic approach using elements from many different methods and strategies to ensure ELLs get the most access to the language arts curriculum and to learning.

Total Physical Response (TPR) is a systematized approach using commands devised by psychologist James Asher (1982). TPR is an effective means of introducing students and adults to a second language. It works on their listening skills in the early developmental stage and works with students who have had no previous exposure to English. Teachers speak a command (for example, "Stand up"), and the students respond physically. The teacher continues with other commands until the activity reaches its end. There is no pressure to speak, so the affective filter is lowered. This is especially useful with beginners who may be in a "silent period."

The Natural Approach, devised by Krashen and Terrell (1983), exposes children to new vocabulary used in meaningful context. Children have extended listening experiences, including TPR, colorful pictures explaining concepts, and active involvement through physical contact with the pictures and objects being discussed. They will make choices, answer yes-no questions, and engage in gamelike situations. For listening comprehension, ELLs conduct meaningful communication and acquire language instead of learning it.

The Whole Language Approach increases linguistic, cognitive, and early literacy skills in an integrated fashion by developing all four language skills: listening, speaking, writing, and reading (Goodman, Goodman, and Hood 1989). This approach incorporates elements from several instructional strategies to further reading and writing skills. The primary strategy is the Language Experience Approach (LEA).

The SIOP model is based upon comprehensible input and builds on background knowledge (Carrell and Eiserhold 1983; Omaggio 1993). Two important components are teacher preparation and instructional indicators or objectives. The SIOP model comprises strategies for classroom organization and emphazies sound instructional delivery techniques.

See also Skills 5.1 and 5.3.

Skill 5.5   Identify major federal and state court decisions, laws, and policies that have affected the education of ELLs

In 1961, due to the large numbers of Cuban children who migrated to Florida, Dade County Public Schools became one of the first school districts to put a major bilingual education program into action. In 1968, Congress passed the Bilingual Education Act, now known as Title VII of the Elementary and Secondary Education Act (ESEA), which provided funding for all school districts to implement programs for LEP[1] students so that they could participate in academic activities. Since then, the Supreme Court ruled favorably in the *Lau v. Nichols* case, which legally required school districts to improve educational opportunities for LEP students.

A 1969 class action suit filed on behalf of the Chinese community in San Francisco alleged that the school district denied "equal educational opportunity" to their children because the classes the children were required to attend were not taught in the Chinese native language. In ***Lau v. Nichols*** (1974), the Supreme Court ruled in favor of the plaintiffs, stating that no student shall be denied "equal access" to any academic program due to "limited English proficiency." The court determined a set of requirements that academic programs must provide.

Related to *Lau v. Nichols*, the Office of the Department of Health, Education, and Welfare created a committee of experts that established guidelines and procedures for local educational groups serving the LEP population. The "Lau Remedies" became guidelines for all states to assist in the academic needs of LEP students and also provided guidelines for "exiting" LEP programs.

In 1998, **Proposition 227** was passed in California, mandating that English learners be taught following a specific pattern. Instruction was to be "overwhelmingly in English," and students were to have immersion classes with sheltered, or structured, English instruction for a maximum of one year. Parents were given the alternative of signing a waiver if they wished their student to receive bilingual education.

Because California currently has more than one-third of the five million English learners in the United States, the proposition had great impact. After five years, the California Department of Education commissioned the American Institute for Research to conduct a study of the results of Proposition 227. The following are findings of that study:

- The performance gap between ELLs and other students remained constant over the five years of the study. This finding is significant because during the period in question there was a substantial increase in the number of ELLs participating in statewide testing.
- The likelihood of an ELL student reclassifying to English-proficient status after 10 years in California schools is less than 40 percent.
- The methods recommended by Proposition 227 have been shown to have no significant impact on the success of ELLs.

The recommendation of the study was that schools put less emphasis on specific methods and focus more on rewarding academic success and implementing appropriate interventions when failure occurs (Parrish 2006).

Section (9) of **Title III, the renewed No Child Left Behind Act**, would seem to be in direction opposition to Proposition 227:

(Section 3102. Purposes)

---

[1] The term *Limited English Proficiency (LEP) student* has been replaced in common usage with *English Language Learner (ELL)* in most areas of English Language teaching. Nevertheless, the LEP terminology occurs in older legal documents, lawsuits, and court decisions.

The purposes of this part are:

(8) To hold State educational agencies, local educational agencies, and schools accountable for increases in English proficiency and core academic content knowledge of limited English proficient children by requiring:

(A) Demonstrated improvements in the English proficiency of limited English proficient children each fiscal year; and

(B) Adequate yearly progress for limited English proficient children, including immigrant children and youth, as described in section 1111(b) (2)(B); and

(9) To provide State educational agencies and local educational agencies with the flexibility to implement language instruction educational programs, based on scientifically based research on teaching limited English proficient children, that the agencies believe to be the most effective for teaching English

This demonstrates that the best policies and methods for teaching ELLs remain open to debate, even at the highest levels of policymaking.

LULAC et al. v. State Board of Education Consent Decree (1990) was a major piece of legislation, paving the way for increased LEP education. In 1990, a Consent Decree was entered in the U.S. district court through an agreement between the opposing parties. It provides for the following:

- LEP students must have complete access to academic programs.
- Schools will be compliant in providing academic instruction for LEP students, allowing them to pass final graduation exams and receive a diploma.
- School districts are required to adequately identify LEP students and administer appropriate academic assessment.
- Schools are required to create an LEP Plan to meet the individual needs of each district that is approved by the DOE.
- LEP Plan makes provisions, protecting the constitutional rights of LEP students.
- Access to appropriate curriculum and certified instructors is essential for LEP students, regardless of the instructional system or methodology.

Skill 5.6   **Apply the sections and requirements of the *League of United Latin American Citizens (LULAC) et al. v. State Board of Education* Consent Decree 1990 (1990 Florida Consent Decree) to specific situations**

League of United Latin American Citizens (LULAC) et al. v. State Board of Education resulted in a Consent Decree on August 14, 1990. The Consent Decree constituted Florida's blueprint for compliance with the 10 federal and state laws for accommodating non-native speakers of English or limited English proficiency (LEP) students. The Consent Decree addresses the civil rights of LEP students, specifically their right to equal access to all educational programs as native speakers.

The Consent Decree addresses six sections that specify how instruction is to be implemented for non-native speakers of English.

Section I: Identification and Assessment

All non-native speakers of English must be appropriately identified and their abilities assessed. The Consent Decree outlines

- how the ELL student is to be integrated into English for Speakers of Other Languages (ESOL);
- the procedures for the transition out of an ESOL program; and
- how the students will be monitored once he or she has transitioned out of the ESOL program.

Section II: Equal Access to Appropriate Programming

All Florida public school–enrolled ELL students are entitled to educational programs, which

- support their level of English language proficiency, academic standing, as well as any additional programs designed to support special needs;
- provide instruction in basic subject areas, which are aligned with their level of proficiency with English; and
- ensure that the basic subject areas are equivalent in quality of instruction to those available for non-ELL students.

Section III: Equal Access to Appropriate Categorical and Other Programs for ELL Students

All ELL students are entitled to educational programs that support their individual academic needs, such as early childhood education and vocational and adult programs. These programs will be appropriately adjusted according to the ELL students' level of English language proficiency.

Other programs, such as dropout prevention and various other support services, shall be made available regardless of the ELL's level of English language proficiency.

Section IV: Personnel

Teachers must have appropriate certification and in-service training to qualify as ESOL instructors. Training may be obtained through a college or university program, as well as in-service training offered through the school district. The Consent Decree outlines the necessary requirements for ESOL certification and ESOL instructor standards.

Section V: Monitoring Issues

To ensure compliance with the provisions of the Consent Decree, the Office of Academic Achievement through Language Acquisition (AALA) within the Florida Department of Education is responsible for monitoring all local school districts.

Section VI: Outcome Measures

The Florida Department of Education is required to develop a system that evaluates the ELL's access to academic programs and to track the program's effectiveness.

Data such as retention, graduation, dropout rates, grade point averages, and state assessment scores of the ELL will be collected and analyzed. Comparisons will then be made between ELL and non-ELL students.

The *LULAC et al. v. State Board of Education* Consent Decree covers the following specific situations: equal educational opportunities, equal access monitoring, compensatory education, exceptional education, dropout prevention, and graduation requirements. Underlying all situations are these two guidelines:

1. All instruction, communication, services, and so on must be aligned with the English language proficiency level of the LEP student.
2. All instruction must be equal in quality, depth, and scope to the instruction made available to native speakers of English.

Equal Educational Opportunities:

Every LEP student has the right to equal access to comprehensive academic programs, in alignment with the student's level of English proficiency, scholarly achievement, and special needs. "Equal access" is not limited to ESOL instructional programs; it includes math, science, social studies, computer proficiency, and special services, such as early childhood, vocational, adult education, extended day care programs, and remedial instruction.

Equal Access Monitoring:

Every three years, the Florida Department of Education reviews each school within the district. The results reveal whether the schools are complying with the Consent Decree (1990) resolutions. Should it be discovered that schools are not in compliance, the school district is notified and requested to make corrections.

COMPETENCY 6.0   **Knowledge of standards-based ESOL and content instruction**

Skill 6.1   **Select methods to improve ELLs' English listening skills for a variety of academic and social purposes**

With respect to listening skills, Ur (1996) lists some of the occasions on which we listen and appropriately respond:

- Interviews
- Instructions
- Loudspeaker announcements
- Radio news
- Committee meetings
- Shopping encounters
- Theater
- Telephone
- Lessons or lectures
- Conversation and gossip
- Television
- Storytelling

Most of these situations use language that is informal and spontaneous. In the classroom, teachers are training ELLs for real-life listening situations. Bearing this in mind, the most useful types of activities are those wherein the listener (ELL) is asked to listen to genuinely informal talk instead of typical written text. The speaker should be visible to the listener, and there should be direct speaker-listener interaction. Finally, there should be only one exposure to the text because in real life the listener rarely will have the opportunity to have the text "replayed."

The tasks themselves should be presented in such a way that the ELL can use his or her previous knowledge to anticipate outcomes. Saying "You are going to hear a husband and wife discuss summer vacation plans" is far more useful than stating, "Listen to the passage . . ." Also, ELLs should be given a task to complete as they listen (e.g., listen for information about where they are planning to go and mark this on their maps). Finally, ELLs should be permitted to answer the questions as they hear the information rather than waiting until the end (adapted from Ur 1996).

Skill 6.2   **Select methods to improve ELLs' English speaking skills for a variety of academic and social purposes**

The following are some of the activities that teachers can do to encourage more oral production from the ELLs in authentic situations:

- Total Physical Response (TPR): Give commands to which students must respond to show understanding. The children's game "Simon Says" may be used with students of all ages by increasing the stakes (e.g., give the commands at faster rate or make them more complex, always keeping in mind the ability level of the ELLs).

- Group work: Encourage authentic language by structuring tasks when ELLs ask for clarification, participate in discussions, interrupt one another, compete for the floor, and kid around. Group work also encourages learner autonomy.

- Task-based activities: Offer activities that require the members of the group to achieve an objective and express it in notes, a rearrangement of jumbled items, a drawing, or a spoken summary.

Ellis (1994: 596–598) concluded that two-way exchanges of information show more benefits:

- Two-way tasks require more negotiation of meaning.
- ELLs usually produce more complex and more target-like language when they have sufficient time to plan their responses.
- Closed tasks (those with a single correct solution) produce more negotiation work than those that have no predetermined solution.

Skill 6.3   Apply standards-based instruction that develops ELLs' oral English in order to support learning in reading and writing English

Oral language development and language skills such as reading, writing, speaking, and listening need to be developed in conjunction with one another. They are all interrelated and integrated.

- **Practice** in any one area promotes development in the other areas.
- **Connections** between abstract and concrete concepts are best made when all language processes are incorporated and integrated during practice and application.

English language learners benefit from opportunities to use English in multiple settings. Learning is more effective when students have an opportunity to participate fully, actively discussing ideas and information. Through meaningful interaction, students can practice speaking and making themselves understood by asking and answering questions, negotiating meaning, clarifying ideas, and other techniques. These activities require ELLs to use the four language skills (reading, writing, speaking, and listening) to successfully complete each task.

Opportunities for Interaction

- Effective teachers strive to provide a balanced linguistic exchange between themselves and their students.
- Interaction accesses the thought processes of another and solidifies one's own thinking.
- Talking with others, either in pairs or small groups, allows for oral rehearsal of learning.

It is important to encourage students to elaborate on their verbal responses and challenge them to go beyond "yes" and "no" answers:

- Tell me more about that."
- "What do you mean by . . .?"
- "What else . . .?"
- "How do you know?"

It also is important to allow wait time for students to formulate answers. If necessary, the teacher can call on another student to extend his or her classmate's response.

All students, including English language learners, benefit from instruction that frequently includes a variety of grouping configurations. It is recommended that at least two different grouping structures be used during a lesson. Here are two examples:

- **Flexible small groups**
  o To promote multiple perspectives
  o To encourage collaboration

- **Partnering**
  o To provide practice opportunities
  o To scaffold instruction
  o To give assistance before independent practice

Additionally, teachers should provide activities that allow interaction with varied student groupings.

- Group students homogeneously by language proficiency, language background, and/or ability levels.
- Heterogeneous variety maintains students' interest.
- Movement from whole class, to partners, to small group increases student involvement.
- Heterogeneous grouping can challenge students to a higher level and provide good student models.
- Varying group structures increases the preferred mode of instruction for students.

Cooperative Learning Ideas

- **Information gap activities**
  Each student in a group has only one or two pieces of the information needed to solve the puzzle or problem. Students must work together, sharing information, while practicing their language and using critical thinking skills.
- **Jigsaw**
  Jigsaw a reading task by chunking text into manageable parts (one to two pages). Students pool their information.
- **Roundtable**
  Use with open-ended questions and grammar practice. Small groups of students sit at tables with one sheet of paper and a pencil. The teacher gives each group a question, concept, or problem; students pass paper around table, each writing his or her own response. Teacher circulates room.

- **3-Step Interview**
  Students are paired. Each student listens to the other as they respond to a topic question. At the end of three minutes, each pair joins another pair of students and shares what their partners said. This activity provides students with a good way to practice language.
- **Writing Headlines**
  This activity provides a way to practice summarizing an activity, story, or project. Teacher provides models of newspaper or magazine headlines. Students work in pairs writing a headline for an activity. Pairs share their headlines with the rest of the class, and the class votes on the most effective headlines.

Wait Time

Wait time varies by culture. Research has shown that the average amount of wait time in American classrooms is not sufficient. Teachers should

- allow students to express their thoughts fully and without interruption; and
- allow students to discuss their answers with a partner before sharing with the whole group.

Skill 6.4   **Apply appropriate standards-based reading instruction for ELLs at varying English proficiency levels**

The International Reading Association (1997) issued a position statement on the place of phonics in reading instruction. This position paper asserts that phonics has an important place in beginning reading instruction, if primary teachers value and teach phonics and effective phonics practice is integrated into the total language arts program. To help children learn phonics, teaching analytical phonics in context seems to work better than teaching synthetic phonics in isolation (for example, on worksheets).

Some of the techniques for beginning reading development, skills, and strategies are noted below:

- Teaching children to understand sentences, texts, and other materials is better than trying to teach the word skills in isolation.
- Children can learn the alphabet principles by alphabetizing lists of spelling words or groups of objects.
- Simple techniques such as holding up the left hand and recognizing the letter 'L' can help children remember on which side of the text to begin reading.
- Learning to decode words is best achieved by practicing while reading.
- Sight words can be memorized.
- Three major types of context clues are syntactic (word order, word endings, function of words in a sentence), semantic (meaning clues), and phonemes and graphemes (/ph/ may sound like /f/, as in *photograph*; /ch/ sometimes sounds like a /k/, as in *chemistry*).
- Reading fluency may be improved by observing the following strategies: Reread for clarity and to improve understanding, ask for help when confused, realize that "there is no such thing as a stupid question." Venn diagrams, webs, and other graphics may be helpful in organizing texts for easier understanding.

- Vocabulary cards or dictionaries may help ELLs recall words they don't know. Word walls and instruction on idioms, antonyms, synonyms, and homonyms are useful.
- Learning the structure of sentence patterns, question forms, and punctuation can help the ELL determine meaning.

Vocabulary

Research has shown that the same 1,000 words (approximately) make up 84 percent of the words used in conversation and 74 percent of the words in academic texts (*The Nation* 2001). The second most frequently used 1,000 words increases the percentages to 90 percent of the words used in conversation and 78 percent used in academic texts. The ELL needs to understand 95 percent to achieve comprehension of the academic text. ELLs need to acquire the 2,000 most used words and work on academic content words at the same time. To help students acquire the vocabulary they need for school, consider the following:

- Vocabulary development for young children is increased using the same methods used with native speaker beginning readers: ample exposure to print, word walls, realia, signs on objects around the room, and so on.
- Older children may take advantage of all these methods in addition to studying true and false cognates, creating personal dictionaries, journal writing between themselves and their teacher, and using learning strategies to augment their vocabulary.
- The following are other strategies from Peregoy and Boyle (2008):
  o Activate the prior knowledge of the ELL.
  o Repeat the new word in meaningful contexts.
  o Explore the word in depth through demonstrations, direct experience, concrete examples, and applications to real life.
  o Have students explain concepts and ideas in writing and speaking using the new words.
  o Provide explicit strategy instruction so that students can independently understand and use the new words.

Fluency is developed over time through extensive practice with both speaking and reading. ELLs should have ample opportunities to develop their speaking and listening abilities to help them achieve more oral fluency. Role-plays, skits, poems, singing, and telephone dialogs are good ways to increase oral fluency. Fluency in reading interacts with oral fluency. Wide exposure to print and reading will increase both reading fluency and oral fluency. The two are intertwined.

Fluent readers are able to grasp chunks of language, read for meaning (and not word by word), and decode automatically. They are confident readers who are able to self-monitor and maintain comprehension. Specific instruction devoted to these areas should improve fluency rates in slower readers.

Second language teaching (SLT) recognizes the importance of giving ELLs integrative tasks that further their language goals by including any or all of the following language skills: listening, speaking, reading, writing, and viewing. Tasks are loosely defined as any activity that emphasizes meaning over form. Which tasks are chosen depends on the teacher who makes decisions about appropriate tasks for his or her classroom.

Literacy is a complex set of skills that comprise the interrelated processes of reading and writing. Reading requires decoding, accurate and fluent word recognition, and comprehension at the word, phrase, sentence, and text levels. Writing requires automatic letter formation and/or keyboarding, accurate and fluent spelling, sentence construction, and the ability to compose a variety of different text structures with coherence and cohesion.

Literacy involves the integration of speaking, listening, and critical thinking. Young children use their oral language skills to learn to read, while older children use their reading ability to further their language learning. The instructional components necessary for reading and writing include: phonemic awareness, phonics, vocabulary building, fluency development, comprehension, text structure, and writing process strategies, as well as prerequisite writing skills such as handwriting, spelling, and grammar.

A survey of research points to the following indicators of effective instructional literacy practices:

- Motivating students according to their unique needs and interests
- Providing direct, explicit instruction of reading and writing skills and strategies based on ongoing student assessment
- Modeling the effective thinking skills that good readers and writers employ
- Devoting 50 percent of the students' instructional time on a daily basis to reading and writing in the classroom
- Activating students' prior knowledge to help them make connections between what they know and what they would like to learn (e.g., KWL)
- Providing opportunities for students to make text and writing connections to their lives, forms of media, and the world
- Offering both guided and independent reading experiences
- Differentiating instruction with a plentiful supply of multilevel books to accommodate interests and ability levels
- Motivating readers by offering a choice of books to read that are at their independent reading level and that they can read with accuracy, fluency, and comprehension
- Promoting conversation through purposeful and guided discussion about a book, piece of writing, or topic
- Guiding discussions through open-ended questioning
- Creating a personable learning environment
- Designing projects that excite and engage students (integration of subjects) as opposed to engaging in short, disconnected tasks
- Assessing student work based on common rubrics

Skill 6.5   **Apply appropriate standards-based writing instruction for ELLs at varying English proficiency levels**

It is crucial to teach the **writing process**; many students come from backgrounds in which their concept of writing a text or paper is very different from the U.S. conventions. These students may be unfamiliar with the concept of planning the paper, doing research, organizing the material, developing a thesis statement, deciding on methods of development, drafting, revising, and editing. Teachers can devise rubrics that are appropriate to process writing and take into consideration both the process and the product.

There are many ways to get students to practice writing without grading the writing; for example, learning logs, journals, and quick-writes. Teachers can devise prompts that allow the ELLs to reflect on their learning and class discussions or explore new ideas. They may rewrite complex ideas in their own words and compare, evaluate, critique, or interpret. At the end of the period, students may quickly write what they learned during the class. ELLs can write dialog either in pairs or individually. They can try using vocabulary words from their text in comprehensible paragraphs. They also can write from the perspective of another person, place, or thing (adapted from Zwiers 2007).

Other students may be fairly sophisticated in their manipulation of language. However, their language may value aspects of writing that are different from the U.S. idea of a sentence (SVO) or a paragraph (the topic sentence and its supporting details). When teaching essay writing, teachers must skillfully model the idea of developing sentences of varying lengths and structures and connecting them through the careful use of connectors, integrating many examples into the instruction. Ample resources, such as dictionaries and lists of vocabulary conventions or connectors, will be invaluable to ELLs in upper levels.

Also, students who are learning to write need to read as much as possible of the genre in which they are going to be writing. Because writing takes place in multiple genres (such as narrative prose, poetry, mathematical proofs, historical accounts, case studies, essays, emails, and letters), students should be exposed to each particular type of writing—its organization, the thinking behind the form, the grammar, and the terms used in each genre—so that they are able to replicate the appropriate phrases and syntax in their writing. Because nonmainstream students will not have had as much exposure to the models as native speakers, it is necessary to point out the conventions of each genre as it is studied in the classroom.

Skill 6.6 **Select methods to develop ELLs' writing through a range of activities from sentence formation to extended writing (e.g., expository, narrative, persuasion)**

Rhetorical Patterns Used in English

Academic English usually is developed using one of the following strategies of development and arrangement of ideas. (There are many exceptions to these arrangements.)

STRATEGIES FOR DEVELOPMENT	PURPOSES	ARRANGEMENT OF IDEAS
Description	Reporting on individual features of a particular subject. • Uses sensory details for support and spatial order	Spatial order
Narration	Studying the changes of a subject over a period of time. Used to • tell a story or incident; • explain a process; or • explain cause and effect.	Chronological order
Classification	Analyzing a subject in relationship to others using one of three methods: • Dividing • Defining • Comparing and contrasting	Logical order
Evaluation	Judging the value of a subject. Used to • inform people; or • persuade them to act or think differently about the topic.	Order of importance

By observing the purposes of the development in different types of prose, students can develop their writing. There are numerous conventions and standard phrases the teacher can introduce to make the process easier.

Here are some examples of the types of phrases used in writing for different purposes.

Descriptive phrases
  • He wore a red jacket and white sneakers.
  • The spaceship took off from Cape Canaveral in a cloud of smoke.

Narrative phrases
- Once upon a time . . .
- Yesterday, my father . . .
- First, mix the sugar and butter together
- When it rains a lot, rivers become full and may cause flooding.

Classification phrases
- The students are tall, short, or in between.
- When I say ELLs, I generally mean students who . . . ,
- The dolphin is a mammal like the whale, but it is much smaller in size.

Evaluation phrases
- The State Board of Education has ruled that students . . .
- After a long and harsh summer in Florida, wouldn't you like to visit the mountains and enjoy a cooler climate?

Students can be taught typical phrases to use for specific pieces of writing. The best examples come from published writers who are experts at different types of writing, so extensive reading is excellent preparation for writing tasks.

Skill 6.7	**Select activities, tasks, and assignments that develop authentic uses (e.g., real-world, contextualized) of English language and literacy to assist ELLs in learning academic language and content-area material**

Task-based learning is based upon the work of Prabhu (1983). Prabhu found that students learn best when presented with tasks that involve investigating their own community for solutions to specific assignments.

- An example is having students read about recycling. After reading about recycling, they would investigate how recycling is used in their community. By interviewing their parents to see how they recycle in their homes or interviewing other members of the community, students are using real-world, contextualized language. Other elements of the assignment could be pre-teaching the vocabulary, including a concluding activity such as a written summary, having discussions in peer groups, and watching a film on the subject.
- Students could collect information about local restaurants and practice ordering from different menus.
- Students could use promotional materials from tourist bureaus to plan a dream trip to a theme park.

See also Skill 5.2.

Skill 6.8   **Select instruction that effectively integrates listening, speaking, reading, and writing for ELLs at varying English proficiency levels**

A number of program models involving the integration of language and content instruction have been developed to meet the needs of language-minority students. In this approach, the second, or foreign, language is used as the medium of instruction for mathematics, science, social studies, and other academic subjects; it is the vehicle used for teaching and acquiring subject-specific knowledge. The focus of the second language classroom should be on something meaningful, such as academic content. Modification of the target language facilitates language acquisition and makes academic content accessible to second language learners.

Integrated language and content instruction enables English as a Second Language (ESL) students to continue their academic and cognitive development while acquiring academic language proficiency. In **theme-based programs**, a language curriculum is developed around selected topics drawn from one content area (e.g., marketing) or from across the curriculum (e.g., pollution and the environment). The theme could be a week or two long and should focus on language taught in a meaningful way. The goal is to assist learners in developing general academic language skills through interesting and relevant content. There are a variety of strategies to teach the integrated approach to language teaching. The following are the four most important of these (Crandall 1994):

- **Cooperative learning:** In this method, students of different linguistic and educational backgrounds and different skill levels work together on a common task for a common goal pertaining to the content being taught in the classroom. The focus also is on an implicit or explicit language feature that the students acquire through negotiation of meaning.

- **Task-based or experiential learning:** Appropriate contexts are provided for developing thinking and study skills and language and academic concepts for students at different levels of language proficiency. Students learn by carrying out specific tasks or projects that they complete with a focus on the content, but they also learn language and academic skills.

- **Whole language approach:** The philosophy of whole language is based on the concept that students need to experience language as an integrated whole. It focuses on an integrated approach to language instruction within a context that is meaningful to students (Goodman 1986). The approach is consistent with integrated language and content instruction, because both emphasize meaningful engagement and authentic language use and both link oral and written language development (Blanton 1992). Whole language strategies that have been implemented in content-centered language classes include dialogue journals, reading response journals, learning logs, process-based writing, and language experience stories (Crandall 1992).

- **Graphic organizers:** These frameworks provide a "means for organizing and presenting information so that it can be understood, remembered, and applied" (Crandall 1992). Students use graphs, realia, tables, maps, flow charts, timelines, and Venn diagrams to help them place information in a comprehensible context. These props enable students to organize information obtained from written or oral texts, develop reading strategies, increase retention, activate schema as a prereading or prelistening activity, and organize ideas during the prewriting stage (Crandall 1992).

Skill 6.9   **Identify appropriate adaptations of curricular materials and modifications of instruction according to an ELL's level of English proficiency and prior knowledge**

Recent research in the area of instructional design and implementation has made useful insights that could be applied across both grade level and language classroom settings to support ESL students' English language and literacy development. Language and literacy development is the key objective of any grade-level curriculum to ensure success both inside and outside the school setting. These insights can be synthesized into seven key instructional criteria for designing and conducting instruction to support ESL students' language and literacy development (Enright 1991):

- **Collaboration:** Instruction should be organized for students to have many opportunities to interact and work cooperatively with one another and with teachers, family members, and community members. During collaborative activities, teachers and students actively work together for learning to take place. This entails activities that require communicating and sharing, such as discussion groups, student partners, or student-teacher dialogue journals. Collaborative activities also may involve students in interacting with people outside the classroom, such as interviewing the school drama club for the class newspaper or working with a parent or an elder on a project about special family traditions.

- **Purpose:** Instruction is organized so that students have multiple opportunities to use authentic oral and written language to complete tasks for real-life goals and purposes. An example of a purposeful composition and questioning activity would be students writing letters to city officials to invite them to a class election forum and then interviewing them about school issues. There are four major kinds of purposeful discourse that can be used as part of learning activities across the curriculum. These are: (a) shared discourse, in which language is used socially to communicate and share meaning to accomplish social goals (playing games or planning a short scene); (b) fun discourse, in which language is used for fun (singing songs and writing riddles); (c) fact discourse, in which language is used to get new information and concepts (doing a research project); and (d) thought discourse, in which language is used to imagine and create new ideas and experiences (writing poetry or critical thinking). These discourse features ensure that students learn both language and content with clear goals in mind.

- **Student interest:** Instruction is organized to both promote and follow students' interest. The instructional goals are unchanged, but the focus is on organizing activities that combine students' interests and purposes with the curriculum topics and objectives.

- **Previous experience:** Instruction is organized to include students' previous experiences in the new learning. This includes tapping into students' previous language and literacy experiences in their first language, in English and into their already developed knowledge and cultural experiences. This type of activity entails relating new concepts and materials to students' background experiences, such as brainstorming ideas before reading a text or connecting previous class activities to new ones. Examples include: incorporating histories and folktales from ESL students' families and native countries in reading group instruction or having students collect authentic speech and literacy data from their homes and neighborhoods and discussing their findings in class.

- **Support:** Instruction is organized so that students feel comfortable and take risks when using English. The classroom atmosphere should be supportive, providing challenging but safe opportunities for students to learn English. The activities are adapted to students' current language and literacy capabilities or zones of proximal development (Vygotsky 1978) in the second language, providing scaffolding of the newly acquired skills.

- **Variety:** Instruction is organized to include a variety of learning activities and language forms and uses. This means that students are exposed to a wide range of oral and written English that they are expected to use in the classroom and in their daily lives. This organization of variety includes the instructional practices of collaboration, learning purposes, student interests, and familiar and unfamiliar student experiences within classroom learning activities.

- **Integration:** Instruction is organized to integrate the various programs and resources available for supporting ELLs' language and literacy development so that they complement one another. This may include integrating the students' in-school and out-of-school experiences; integrating content and language instruction; integrating the four language skills of reading, writing, listening, and speaking; and integrating the students within the classroom through cooperative learning.

COMPETENCY 7.0   **Knowledge of resources and techniques**

Skill 7.1   **Evaluate and select culturally responsive, age-appropriate, and linguistically accessible materials for ELLs at varying English proficiency levels**

Language-rich environments are crucial for ELLs. No two people learn in the same way, so diverse materials on the same subject may help students bridge the gap between prior knowledge and knowledge to be acquired.

Students with little or no English or previous educational experience may be taught in their native language when possible. Research shows that students who are taught content in their native or heritage language benefit from simultaneous language instruction in English (Slavin and Cheung 2003).

For students who have reached a certain level of competency in English, scaffolding is recommended. ELL students need extra help with vocabulary, linguistic complexities, idioms, prefixes and suffixes, and false cognates. (Teachers who are able can increase ELLs' vocabulary using cognate instruction.)

School media specialists and ESOL specialists are excellent resources for locating particular materials.

See Skill 1.4 for further suggestions.

Skill 7.2   **Evaluate and select a variety of materials and other resources, including L1 resources, appropriate to ELLs' English language and literacy development**

See Skill 7.1.

Skill 7.3   **Apply technological resources (e.g., Internet, software, computers, related media) to enhance language and content-area instruction for ELLs at varying English proficiency levels**

In today's society, the explosion of technology has given most school-age children ample opportunities to explore the world of technology on their own. Students are Internet, game, Twitter, and Facebook savvy. In the case of ELLs, this may or may not be true. Teachers should make every effort to provide equal access to the technology available at the school and district level.

Computer-assisted language learning (CALL) has tremendous positive implications for creating highly individualized, interactive, and meaningful learning experiences and simulation exercises. Instead of having to create tests, question banks, practice exercises, and remedial curriculum, instructors now have access to these components through CALL. Furthermore, the instructor can tailor the instruction to the learner's individual needs rather than interrupting the learning process of the entire class. Typically, these software programs also integrate a computerized "grade book," which allows the instructor to track the learner's progress and scores.

In terms of testing learners, instructors can not only create individualized tests but also take advantage of randomization features, which protect the integrity of the testing material.

CALL even integrates feedback into the instruction. Learners can receive useful feedback in response to their interaction with the software and then branch off limitlessly, depending on their interests and needs. Nagata and Swisher (1995) demonstrated that "computer-mediated feedback, which recognizes and offers meaningful language practice is beneficial to learners at the sentence level" (Shrum and Glisan 2000).

According to researchers (Alderson 2000; Brown 1997; Dunkel 1999), the following factors diminish the practicality of CALL: computer-generated feedback for measuring the accuracy of the learners' speaking ability is not reliable; learners who were not computer-literate were disadvantaged; and the testing was limited by the lack of context.

Computer-mediated communication (CMC) is considered more appropriate for writing than for speaking because all input and output happens with the keyboard and because learners cannot be assessed for accuracy of pronunciation. It shares many of the qualities of CALL, such as: creating a learner-centered, instead of instructor-centered, environment; offering a variety of interactive and meaningful learning experiences; and tailoring individual sequences of instruction.

Major Research Findings: Computer-Assisted Language Learning (CALL)
Since 1995, CALL has been researched and evaluated to determine its usefulness and effectiveness in SLA. Educators and researchers seek to reap all potential benefits of CALL, such as integrating video and audio into instruction to increase the learner's textual comprehension (Chun and Pass 1997). In 1999, Kramsch and Anderson were in favor of the cultural authenticity brought to life by multimedia. This type of realism provides a language-rich learning environment, second-best to experiencing the culture first hand. The possibilities for integrating CALL into mainstream instruction are less and less limited. For example, some proponents like Eshani and Knodt (1998) and James (1996) see potential in CALL for voice recognition, which could develop the learners' speaking skills.

For instructors, CALL has enormous potential because certain authoring software tools have features for creating computer-based course materials that require no programming skills on the instructors' part and are not cost-prohibitive, such as Hypercard from Macintosh.

Major Research Findings: Computer-mediated Communication (CMC)
Computer-mediated Communication (CMC) is different from CALL in that CALL programs are typically individual in nature. Whereas CMC is "socially friendly" and offers a forum for online interaction, which potentially can be a significant source of support and collaboration between learners. For instance, email, chat rooms, list-serves, etc. provide "very realistic form[s] of communication because it is a real conversation about real, relevant topics with real people" (Kroonenberg 1994/95).

Types of computer learning
Russell (1997) compared traditional classroom courses with distance studies and found no significant difference although there was considerable variation.

Machtmes and Asher (2000) analysis of video-based distances courses (telecourses) found that two-way communication between the instructor and the students was more effective than traditional courses.

Asynchronous Learning:
Interchange is an asynchronous application, which permits learners to communicate in real-time. As an instructional tool, it has gained popularity because L2 learners can communicate with speakers in the TL; and as the L2 learner has a socially internalized motivation to participate and communicate effectively, the learning experience itself becomes highly meaningful.

Then too, remember that Florida is a nationally recognized leader in K-12 virtual education. Florida has the largest state virtual school in the nation and Florida school districts offer online schools, programs and/or courses for their students. Florida's virtual schools and programs provide high quality online instruction and curriculum that meet state and national standards and are held accountable for student and school/program performance (fldoe.org). These courses may be an alternative for some ELL students.

Skill 7.4   **Identify effective means of collaboration with school-based, district, and community resources to advocate for equitable access for ELLs**

In *Plyler v. Doe,* 457 U.S. 202, the U.S. Supreme Court ruled that all children, regardless of immigration status, have the right to free public education by claiming the benefit of the Equal Protection Clause of the Fourteenth Amendment. Such children have the right to appropriate academic services, free breakfast and lunch, transportation, and the opportunity to apply to different schools, including high schools and gifted and talented programs. The League of United Latin American Citizens, or LULAC, keeps a vigilant watch over how the state implements its education programs for children still learning English.

By advocating for the ELL, the ESOL instructor can ensure that the students in his or her charge are able to participate in the school band, science club, math club, chess club, sports teams, and all other activities in which students of their age and inclination participate.

Encouraging students and their families to make full use of public resources such as the local public library—including its online resources—will help them expand their knowledge and understanding of resources available to English language learners. In addition, many libraries have afterschool, Saturday, or holiday programs to encourage constructive use of students' time.

Museums also often have educational outreach programs that all citizens may use. Other resources, such as parks and the local YMCA and YWCA (or similar organizations), offer recreational facilities to all citizens.

See also Skill 1.6.

Skill 7.5   **Identify major professional organizations, publications, and resources that support continuing education for teachers**

See Skill 1.4.

COMPETENCY 8.0   **Knowledge of planning standards-based instruction to ELLs**

Skill 8.1   **Apply appropriate language objectives and state-approved content-based standards to plan instruction for ELLs at varying English proficiency levels**

Cummins (1981) observed that the academic language of the content areas prevents many ELLs from achieving success in school, so instruction in the native or heritage language may be an appropriate option for beginning English language learners. Krashen and Biber (1988) believed that comprehensible input is a critical element in effective instruction in English. However, by combining content instruction with English as the medium of instruction, ELLs can learn impressive amounts of English and their content materials. Both methods are valid and are supported by the Consent Decree (1990).

The Consent Decree (1990) requires that instruction always be understandable for ELLs, though it does not require that any specific instructional model or approach be used. The two major approaches in achieving this are using ESOL strategies to deliver instruction and using English and the heritage (native) language to deliver instruction.

When using ESOL strategies, school personnel must be sure of the following:

- All subject matter is in conformity with the use of ESOL strategies for teaching ELLs basic subject matter and such techniques are used at all times so that the ELLs understands what is being taught.
- Each class is taught by qualified instructors and appropriate materials are available.
- All students are progressing toward the district's pupil progression plan.
- All ESOL programs must be taught in accordance with the high standards of non-ELLs in the same basic subject areas. Programs should be consistent with the state's required curriculum and student performance standards. If available, the program must provide home language tests and instructional materials.

When using English and the heritage (native) language to deliver content, instructors should remember the following:

- ELLs who speak a language other than English have varying abilities and talents just as English-speaking children do.
- Content-area instruction must be delivered using sound instructional methods that promote both formal and informal registers in the heritage language and in English.
- By developing their heritage language, ELLs become positive members of society who will benefit from the ability to function in two languages all their lives.
- ELLs are capable of speaking, reading, and writing English at the same level as their English-speaking peers.
- Better employment opportunities are available for bilinguals than monolinguals, so ELLs should actively develop language literacy in both languages.

Skill 8.2 **Identify the characteristics of engaging, challenging, and collaborative student-centered classroom environments for diverse learners**

Teachers should take care when using **ability grouping**. *An Imperiled Generation* (1988) by the Carnegie Foundation reported on the harmful effects of ability grouping. This is still true today. Ability grouping

- carries a social stigma;
- promotes negative feelings about school by low achievers;
- hinders academic progress for average and low achievers; and
- often widens the gap between high- and low-achieving students.

Slavin's research (2003) shows that both low achievers and high achievers can benefit from mixed-ability cooperative learning groups that hold individuals accountable for achieving group goals. Low achievers are more challenged, improve their self-image, and are more willing to learn.

The following are key features of group learning projects:

- Arranging the classroom furniture to ensure group interaction
- Assigning students to groups to ensure a mixture of genders, ethnicities, linguistic levels, and academic levels
- Meaningful tasks
- Stating objectives as group objectives and precisely clarifying expectations
- Assigning each student a role or job
- Monitoring group work during the task
- Assessing both the individual and group achievements

See also Skill 1.5.

Skill 8.3 **Choose appropriate differentiated learning experiences for lesson planning based on students' English proficiency levels**

In the inclusion classroom, ELLs may be given materials that are adapted for their skill levels and/or they may have an ESOL teacher or aide when available. All vocabulary and language concepts should be taught using high-interest activities.

Teachers should keep in mind that ELLs who are given adapted materials may not know the Roman alphabet and may have to learn it (e.g., students from countries such as Saudi Arabia and Korea). Even when the ELLs are familiar with the Roman alphabet, the letter/sound correspondence may not be the same as in their first language. In Spanish, for example, the letter /g/ can be pronounced three different ways: like an /h/ in *gema* and *girasol*; like a hard /g/ in *gato* and *gramatica*; or like a /w/ in *agua*.

Spanish speakers have difficulty pronouncing the /th/ in English and the numerous ways English vowels can be pronounced. This affects their listening, writing, and pronunciation skills as well as their work in the content areas. Other decoding skills also will need special attention. Teachers will need to address all of these areas for the ELLs to succeed in the general education class.

ELLs whose cultural or ethnic background is different may need explanations of the typical American holidays. Halloween, Thanksgiving, and Christmas all occur within the first few months of the school year. For children from different backgrounds, teachers will have to both adapt materials and explain the holidays.

Teachers also will have to activate ELLs' background knowledge before introducing reading content. They should give ELLs permission to use translating dictionaries in content areas to understand new content or confirm previous knowledge.

Teachers can use peer tutoring by seating students in problem-solving work groups. Mix ability levels in both content areas and language ability so that all students to benefit. Frequently, ELLs do well in mathematics because mathematic symbols are the same or similar in native cultures, but because of language difficulties they may have difficulty working word problems.

Try to avoid abstract problems in the lower grades, especially by relating math and science problems to the real world. Use manipulatives and visual aids to make problems more concrete and realistic.

See also Skill 4.3.

Skill 8.4   **Choose appropriate learning tasks for students with limited L1 literacy and/or limited formal schooling**

The teacher needs to have a variety of ways to model and provide opportunities for guided and independent practice to achieve language and content objectives. For example, teaching the numbers from 1 to 10 to a pre-beginning class could be done in the following way:

- Show the numerals and pronounce the words. Have students repeat the pronunciation.
- Say the numerals in mixed-up order and ask students to hold up the correct number of fingers.
- Dictate the numerals in mixed-up order and ask students to write the numeral they hear.
- Ask selected students to tell the teacher their phone numbers (or a made-up phone number if they don't want to reveal the real one) and write the number on the board as it is spoken.
- Using the telephone directory, students dictate 5 to 10 real telephone numbers to each other, working with a partner. The partner watches and corrects what the other student writes.
- After practicing the question, "What's your phone number?" the students ask as many classmates as possible and write their responses.
- The teacher then asks the class, "What is Carolina's phone number?" and someone other than Carolina responds while the rest of the students verify the response.

Skill 8.5   **Identify methods of scaffolding and providing context for ELLs' learning**

Scaffolding, or supporting children of all ages, consists of demonstrating, guiding, and teaching in a step-by-step process while ELLs are trying to communicate effectively and develop their language skills (Cazden 1983; Ninio and Bruner 1976).

The amount of scaffolding depends on the support needed and the individual child. It allows the ELL to assume more and more responsibility as he or she is able. Once the ELLs feel secure in their abilities, they are ready to move on to the next stage.

Educational scaffolding consists of several linked strategies, including modeling academic language and contextualizing academic language using visuals, gestures, and demonstrations to help students while they are involved in hands-on learning. Some efficient scaffolding techniques are: providing direction, clarifying purpose, keeping the student on task with proposed rubrics that clarify expectations, offering suggestions for resources, and supplying a lesson or activity without problems.

Tompkins (2006) identified five levels of scaffolding for learning and problem solving to show how ELLs move from needing considerable support to the independent level where they are ready to solve problems on their own.

- **Modeling:** The instructor models orally or through written supports (a paragraph, a paper, an example) the work expected of the ELL. Projects from previous years can provide examples of the type of work expected.

- **Shared:** ELLs use their pooled knowledge of the project (and that of their teacher) to complete the assignment.

- **Interactive:** The teacher allows ELLs to question him or her on points on which they need clarification or do not understand. This demonstrates that everyone is a learner. It is especially satisfying for the students when the teacher admits that he or she does not know the answer and helps the students locate it.

- **Guided:** Well-posed questions, clues, reminders, and examples are all ways of guiding the ELL toward the goal.

- **Independent:** The learner achieves independence and no longer needs educational scaffolding.

Skill 8.6   **Identify situations in which reteaching is necessary and appropriate for ELLs**

Fossilization (Selinker 1972) occurs when a learner has reached a good level of communication and is no longer worried about making mistakes. Fossilized errors are habits of speech and are rarely corrected. Therefore, ELLs do not improve despite repeated instruction. The ELLs repeatedly use certain incorrect pronunciation and vocabulary items and make certain grammar mistakes. It becomes very difficult to eliminate these mistakes because they become part of the ELL's newly acquired interlanguage. One very common example of this is the omission of the final /s/ on the third-person singular verbs. However, this usually does not create confusion with meaning because English requires a subject for each verb.

Therefore, ne method for dealing with errors of this type is to ignore them when they do not interfere with meaning and concentrate on the content being taught. Also, it is easier to ignore the incorrect oral speech and work on the mistakes in written work. Frequently, the ELL does not "hear" the spoken error even if it is recorded. In written work, the instructor has a visible source of the student's error with which to work. The instructor can provide mini-lessons for the individual in the hopes that future work (both spoken and written) will be self-edited.

Another strategy is to use peer correction of written work after teaching specific items such as subject-verb agreement. Once the items have been taught in mini-lessons, they may be incorporated into individual or group checklists. Since writing is a process, mechanical details can be peer edited in several revisions after students feel they have achieved their personal goals of self-expression, style, and content.

A third activity is dictation of sentences in English containing sources of frequent error patterns. By showing the structures correctly, many students realize that they say something different and are amazed that this is the correct way to state the sentence.

Sometimes acting like you don't understand, especially with incorrect verb tenses, may help the learner understand that his or her structures are wrong and need work. For example, if the learner says, "I went to my house after school every day," the teacher could say, "Where do you go now? Did you move in with your Grandmother?"

Finally, encourage reading and writing. As students become more proficient in these two areas, they will be better at communicating.

Ellis, in *The Study of Second Language Acquisition*, suggests that "certain error types are not susceptible to de-fossilization." So, teachers may have to ask themselves: Is it worth it? If the errors don't interfere with communication, it may be wiser to celebrate communication and ignore the inevitable.

COMPETENCY 9.0   **Knowledge of assessment issues for ELLs**

Skill 9.1   **Identify factors such as cultural and linguistic bias that affect the assessment of ELLs**

Certain factors may affect the assessment of ELLs who are not familiar with assessment in the U.S. or Florida classroom. Among these is unfamiliarity with standard testing techniques. Students may become disconcerted when they are not allowed to ask questions of the teacher, are restricted by time constraints, or are permitted to work only on certain sections of the test at a time.

Students, both ELLs and non-ELLs, may be uncomfortable when ELLs are allowed specific accommodation during the test session. Accommodations allowed by the test publisher or those prescribed by the State of Florida need to be introduced in the regular classroom so that ELLs and other students are familiar with them before the testing session begins.

Avalos (in Schumm, *Reading Assessment and Instruction for All Learners*, 2006) states that there are four types of bias that can affect validity:

- **Cultural bias:** This bias concerns acquired knowledge from participating in and sharing certain cultural values and experiences. Asking questions about birthdays or holiday celebrations presumes a middle-class family experience. Immigrants frequently do not celebrate birthdays, perhaps because they live in poverty or perhaps because they celebrate the birthday differently (for example, with an extended family and piñatas).
- **Attitudinal bias:** This refers to the negative attitude of the examiner toward a certain language, dialect, or culture. Just as low expectations from instructors can cause low results (the Pygmalion effect), a negative attitude conveyed by the assessor, teacher, or school culture during testing can have negative effects on the test results.
- **Test bias or norming bias:** This type of bias refers to excluding ELLs or other populations from the school's population used to obtain the norm results.
- **Translation bias:** This occurs when the test is literally translated from L2 to L1 by interpreters or other means. The essence of the test may be lost in such translation because it is difficult to translate cultural concepts.

Instructors of LEP students need to be aware of the **less obvious cultural and linguistic bias in tests**, such as students who are unfamiliar with the test-taking techniques of multiple-choice questions and/or bubble answer sheets.

The debate about the fairness and/or cultural bias often associated with standardized tests for assessment seems to be particularly relevant for ELL learners. Some have argued that the "very use of tests is unfair, because tests are used to deprive people of color of their place in society" (Díaz-Rico and Weed 1995). However, the use of such testing as an assessment tool for ELL learners is standard and will continue to be so into the foreseeable future. That being said, the following factors can affect how a test or assessment is administered to the ELL learner and should be taken into consideration:

Anxiety: Testing anxiety for an ELL may go well beyond what is considered "normal" anxiety for a native English speaker. ELLs potentially are at a great disadvantage, not only because they have anxiety about studying for a test but also because the test format itself could be unfamiliar, depending on the ELLs' culture and previous test-taking experience. Multiple-choice questions and especially "cloze," or fill-in-the-blanks, can be intimidating because such formats may not be a true indicator of the ELLs' level of ELL proficiency (Díaz-Rico and Weed 1995.) A potential workaround to reduce the ELLs' anxiety would be to administer practice tests to allow the ELL to develop a comfort level.

Time limitations: The time limitations to which L1 learners in the United States typically are accustomed may create issues for ELLs of other cultures, especially Europe. In the United States, it is customary for the instructor to assign a class period to complete an exam or for L1 learners to take statewide school achievement tests, which are timed in a nonnegotiable fashion and do not allow the learner to skip forward or go back while taking the test. ELLs may need additional time, depending on their comfort level and experience.

Instructor/learner rapport: If the ELL does not have a comfortable relationship with the instructor and/or there are significant language barriers between them, the ELL may not be forthcoming about any questions or clarification about the test. Without the ability or comfort level to address these issues, the ELL's success could be compromised before the test begins. Furthermore, nuances of the English language, idiomatic phrasing, and confusing instructions also can negatively impact the ELL's test performance.

Troublesome testing content: Achievement tests for measuring abilities other than language may contain cultural biases or incorrect translations, which can comprise the scoring for the ELL. For example, some words tend to be lost in translation, such as the word "belfry" in English and its corresponding word in Spanish, which is "campanario." "Belfry" is not common in everyday language use; it usually is found in classic literature. However, "campanario" is commonly used in Spanish. The ELL's overall achievement on such a test could be greatly diminished by unequal translation.

In addition to the above-mentioned factors, cultural and linguistic bias often occurs in tests in other ways.

For example, the story in English-language culture generally has a hero and a villain. The lead character is proactive, assertive, and in search of a goal for which he or she will be rewarded (a pot of gold, the charming prince, or a safe haven). In a Japanese story, the main character's adventures come through chance or fate. His or her rewards come from the kindness or goodness demonstrated throughout the story. Therefore, cultural bias in the story text may lead to testing bias.

The structure of English discourse usually is straightforward. The story starts at Point A and continues until it reaches Point Z. There are very few digressions. Many cultures, however, have discourse styles that are very different. Certain cultural amenities (for example, sipping tea as a prelude to business) must be conducted in both speech and writing in certain cultures. To go straight from Point A to Point Z could show rudeness (for example, in Japanese culture) or a total lack of writing ability (for example, in Spanish culture, in which an author often demonstrates his or her linguistic abilities with verbosity).

Skill 9.2   **Evaluate formal and informal assessment to measure oral language, literacy, and academic achievement**

Teachers have many methods of evaluating their students' oral language. One formal test is the Language Assessment Scales (LAS). It can be used as a diagnostic or placement tool. The oral test has three sections: vocabulary, listening comprehension, and story retelling. The pronunciation component has two parts: minimal sound pairs and phonemes. For a complete picture of the ELL's language abilities, the oral test should be used in conjunction with the LAS reading/writing instrument.

First is the Student Oral Language Observation Matrix (SOLOM). The matrix contains rubrics for assessment in five areas: comprehension, fluency, vocabulary, pronunciation, and grammar. The SOLOM is personalized and allows the teacher to evaluate the student over a period of time and in real-life contexts.

Another method is to use anecdotal observations and checklists, which are more open-ended. Teachers can establish their own specific evaluation needs. These tools are best used during group work or when observing daily classroom performance. Items such as informal talk, reporting, discussing, debating, and reflecting would be appropriate for this type of assessment.

See Skills 11.1 and 11.3 for more information on assessment.

Skill 9.3   **Determine appropriate accommodations during formal and informal assessments of ELLs at varying English language proficiency levels**

When any learners are tested, the main goal is to gather the information necessary for providing them with the most appropriate instruction. As we have seen in the last topic, for ELLs, cultural and linguistic biases exist in testing. The unfortunate result may be that their level of English proficiency and/or achievement in various content areas is reported incorrectly. (This is problematic for both the ELL and the school district, which must test learners to comply with federal legislation, also known as Title 1 or T1. Low test scores sometimes can result in a loss of funding for the school.)

The typical guidelines for testing ELLs are the following:

- *Be tested with certain minor accommodations.**
  *The final decision of when to test and with what accommodations should be made based on each individual ELL.

The following guidelines are accommodations for testing ELLs with at least one year in the T1 environment:

- Give additional time for the ELL to complete the test
- Give permission for the use of a bilingual dictionary
- Read specific parts of the test, as necessary (this accommodation is not appropriate for vocabulary or reading comprehension parts)
- Provide pronunciation and word meaning help

These accommodations are offered to the ELL so that any deficit in the T1 will not cause inaccurate performance results.

Skill 9.4   **Identify characteristics of ELLs with special needs (e.g., speech-language impaired, intellectual disabilities, specific learning disabilities)**

Learning disabilities are defined as physical, emotional, cognitive, or social components that severely limit what is considered to be normal functioning behavior. Children who fall into this category can be one or more of the following: emotionally challenged; hearing, vision, or speech impaired; learning disabled; and so on.

One similarity between second language development and learning disabilities is comprehensive diagnostic testing before placement.

Similarities: Educators have numerous assessment tools to evaluate the proficiency level of an L2 learner. They also have various assessment tools to determine if an L1 learner has a disability, whether it is physical, emotional, or learning. However, assessment tools to determine whether a L2 learner has a learning disability are not currently available. The most reliable method to date is observation and interpretation.

The typical blueprint that L2 learners seem to follow when developing their pronunciation skills can easily be confused with a learning disability, because L2 learners have difficulties with the following areas: omission, substitution, distortion, and addition (Lue 2001). These areas are the same as those encountered by some L1 learners with learning disabilities. The following are examples of the problem areas:

- **Omission:** The L1/L2 learner omits a phoneme (the smallest unit of a word); for example, the L1/L2 learner pronounces "ar" instead of "bar."
- **Substitution:** The L1/L2 learner substitutes a phoneme; for example, the L1/L2 learner pronounces "take" instead of "rake."
- **Distortion:** The L1/L2 learner pronounces a phoneme incorrectly, and the sound produced is not considered normal. For example, the L1/L2 learner pronounces the phoneme "three" as "free."
- **Addition:** The L1/L2 learner adds a syllable to a word. For example, a learner pronounces the word "liked" as "like-id."

Skill 9.5   **Distinguish between the characteristics of ELLs in the natural process of acquiring English and ELLs with specific learning disabilities**

A language disorder is characterized by the learner experiencing difficulties in communication and speech motor skills. Typically, the learner will be noticeably behind his or her classmates in language acquisition or speech skills.

The following summaries outline both the similarities and differences between second language development and language disorders. Remember that an LEP learner who has proficiency in his or her native language but struggles in the L2 environment is *not* considered to have a language disorder.

Similarities:

Some language disorders cause the learner to:

- mispronounce phonemes (the smallest unit of a word);
- have issues with properly identifying a word in context (either verbally or nonverbally);
- have difficulty associating words with their appropriate meanings;
- confuse proper grammatical structures;
- have difficulty understanding advanced vocabulary and
- experience difficulty following directions.

All of these characteristics of language disorders are problems the L2 learner experiences during the process of second language acquisition, the only exception being the problem with following directions. (This falls under language disorders if the learner understands directions but is not cognitively able to follow them.) During the early stages of SLA, L2 learners experience all of the characteristics that are common to language disorders. However, this is due primarily to unfamiliarity with the structure of the L2 language, not to dysfunctions of communication or speech motor skills.

Differences:

The differences between language disorders and second language learning are more distinct than their similarities. First, learners experiencing problems with speech motor skills face the following challenges:

- Unable to produce certain sounds, such as "r" or "l"
- Have voice quality issues (such as pitch or volume)
- Experience "dysfluency," or stuttering
- Experience difficulty creating speech that is understandable to others

Skill 9.6 **Identify characteristics of ELLs who are gifted and talented**

Before a formal referral is given for an ELL, a pre-referral that could circumvent the referral process completely could be an option. When a learner is having academic difficulties in reading and learning, it is necessary to ask the following questions to determine if the contributing factors are related to prior academic training, language, culture, or another variable:

- What are the specific errors the student encounters while reading?
- Could the errors be related to differences between the learner's L1 and L2?
- Does the learner write in a language with non-Roman or non-Latin letters? (For example, Cyrillic has some letters that are very similar to reversed Roman and Latin letters.)
- Are word problems difficult for the ELL? (Word problems typically can be frustrating, because of the wording and the cultural and economic context in which they are placed.)

Bored ELLs

It is common for children who have emigrated from other countries to the United States to lose interest in math tasks, because they previously have mastered the concepts in their native country.

The following are pre-referral questions to ask before identifying such learners as "exceptional":

- Does the subject matter and level of language seem suitable for the learner?
- Are the tasks presented in a clear, simple, and concise manner?
- Are the tasks scaffolded upon the learner's prior knowledge?

Behavioral Issues

ELLs may not respond to the expectations of cultural behaviors in the United States, and this factor alone could cause ELLs to act out. The following are important pre-referral questions to ask:

- Have the classroom and school's expectations regarding appropriate behavior been explained to the ELL? Are the ELL's parents aware as well?
- What is the cultural background of the ELL? Is the ELL from a country in which he or she was exposed to political and civil strife/unrest? Might the ELL be suffering from PTSD (post-traumatic stress disorder)?

Dialect

If the ELL is from a country such as West Africa or India, he or she may have learned English but may speak it with a different or confusing dialect. This is an important pre-referral question to ask:

- How many dialects and languages has the ELL had experience with?

Finally, having an ELL's vision and hearing checked and ruled out as contributing factors, in addition to asking the questions mentioned above, is essential to prevent an unnecessary referral and related extensive assessment and testing.

Exceptional student education (ESE) is a term used in Florida to designate special services for students with disabilities and students who are gifted.

Exceptionality is a special need that qualifies the student for exceptional student education.

Some of the characteristics of students learning a second language seem to be the same as those of students with learning disabilities. This has resulted in an overrepresentation of ELLs in the exceptional groupings (Ortiz and Garcia 1995). While learning another language, students may show apparent processing difficulties, behavioral differences, reading difficulties, and expressive difficulties (Lock and Layton 2002). Only careful observation can determine if these are natural language learning difficulties or, in fact, learning disabilities.

Before students are referred to special education classes, their previous learning experiences should be analyzed using ESOL techniques. Also, any interventions should be documented and implemented for up to 10 weeks (Burnette 1998; Rodriguez and Carrasquillo 1997). The analysis of the results of early intervention strategies should make allowances for typical second language difficulties (Almandos and Petzold 2001).

Teachers should be able to recognize certain characteristics as possible signs of giftedness in LEP students so that when one or more of these are present to a significant degree, the student is referred for screening and possible evaluation.

COMPETENCY 10.0   **Knowledge of language proficiency assessment**

Skill 10.1   **Identify the district, state, and federal requirements for identification, reclassification, and exit of ELLs from ESOL programs**

The Consent Decree is the state of Florida's framework for compliance with the following federal and state laws and jurisprudence regarding the education of English language learner students:

- Title VI and VII Civil Rights Act of 1964
- Office of Civil Rights Memorandum (Standards for Title VI Compliance) of May 25, 1970
- Requirements based on the Supreme Court decision in *Lau v. Nichols*, 1974
- Equal Education Opportunities Act of 1974
- Requirements of the Vocational Education Guidelines, 1979
- Requirements based on the Fifth Circuit court decision in *Castañeda v. Pickard*, 1981
- Requirements based on the Supreme Court decision in *Plyler v. Doe*, 1982
- Americans with Disabilities Act (PL 94-142)
- Florida Education Equity Act, 1984
- Section 504 of the Rehabilitation Act of 1973

Florida's authority for the implementation of the Consent Decree is found in Section 1003.56, F.S., English Language Instruction for Limited English Proficient Students and Rules 6A-6.0900 to 6A-6.0909, F.A.C., Programs for Limited English Proficient Students. (fldoe.org/aala/rules.asp)

See also Skill 5.6.

Title 1 (1965) is a federal program providing funds to states to support extra assistance to students who need help in reading and mathematics.

The No Child Left Behind Act of 2002 (NCLB) requires schools to focus on providing quality education for students who often are overlooked by the educational system: children with disabilities, children from low-income families, non-English speakers, and African Americans and Latinos. It implemented the following regulations, geared specifically for LEP students:

- LEP students are required to be included in all academic assessments that are currently administered to other (non-LEP) students.
- When possible, the assessments must be administered in the language most likely to provide the most accurate data of the student's academic achievement and performance.
- When and if academic assessments in the student's native language cannot be obtained, the state is responsible for developing the appropriate assessment.
- In general, LEP students who have attended U.S. schools (except Puerto Rico) for at least three consecutive years must be administered assessments in English.
- The exception to this last regulation is the following: on an individual-case basis, schools have the option of permitting LEP students an extra two years before the school administers English-based assessments if the school has determined that the LEP student's current level of English proficiency will not provide valid data.
- Parents are to be provided with a detailed report of student achievement, and explanations are provided of achievement levels.

NCLB established general guidelines for classifying ELLs who are entering new schools. In addition to the above-mentioned criteria, the following procedures are typically observed:

ESL students are identified by standardized assessment tests based on a number of factors. Students entering a school for the first time must be given an assessment test of language ability (and parents notified of the results) usually within the first 30 days of the commencement of school. If a student is deemed eligible for ESL services, the ELL begins receiving supplementary language services and is retained in the program until he or she is deemed Fully English Proficient. These students may receive a one-time, one-year deferment from standardized testing to be reported by the school for the purposes of No Child Left Behind legislation.

Each student must be assessed annually in grades 3–8 in Math and Reading/Language Arts. States also must test students once annually in math and reading/language arts in grades 9–12.

| Skill 10.2 | Interpret assessment data from multiple sources to guide instruction for ELLs at varying English proficiency levels |

There are a multitude of tests for evaluating, assessing, and placing ELLs in the appropriate programs. Each test can test a narrow range of language skills (such as discrete tests designed to measure grammar subskills or vocabulary).

A language test should be chosen on the basis of the information it gives, the appropriateness of the instrument for the purpose, and the soundness of the test content. Language has over 200 dimensions that can be evaluated, yet most tests assess fewer than 12 of them. Therefore, all language testing should be done cautiously; backed up by teacher observations, oral interviews, and family life variables; and grounded in school records.

Language placement tests:
A language placement test is designed to place a student within a specific program. The school district may design its own instrument or use a standardized test.

Language proficiency tests:
These tests measure how well students have met certain standards in a particular language. The standards have been predetermined and are unrelated to any course of study, curriculum, or program. These tests frequently are used to enter or exit a particular program.

Examples are

- ACTFL Oral Proficiency Interview (OPI);
- Test of Spoken English (TSE);
- Test of English as a Foreign Language (TOEFL);
- Foreign Service Exam (Foreign Service Institute); and
- Oral Language Proficiency Scale from Miami-Dade County Public Schools.

Language achievement tests:
These tests directly relate to a specific curriculum or course of study. The tests include language subskills, reading comprehension, parts of speech, and other mechanical parts of the language such as spelling, punctuation, and paragraphing.

Examples are

- unit exams; and
- final exams

Diagnostic language tests:
These tests are designed to identify individual students' strengths and weaknesses in languages. They are generally administered by speech therapists or psychologists in clinical settings when specific language learning problems are present.

Skill 10.3	**Identify effective ways to communicate with stakeholders (e.g., primary caregivers, school and district staff, community members) about assessment outcomes that guide policy and instructional practice**

The Florida Department of Education's Public Schools Division maintains webpages with information on Initiatives for Curriculum, Instruction, and Student Services; Student Achievement; Virtual Education; Educator Quality; Early Learning; and Just Read, Florida!

Based on LULAC, each school district is required to establish Parent Leadership Councils (PLC) to accommodate parents of ELLs. A main purpose of these groups is to inform parents about their child's education and instructional practices based on the results of various assessments.

See also Skill 1.6.

COMPETENCY 11.0   **Knowledge of classroom-based assessment for ELLs**

Skill 11.1   **Identify appropriate use of alternative assessments (e.g., authentic, performance-based, peer- and self-assessments) to evaluate content-area learning for ELLs at varying English proficiency levels**

Peer Assessment:
Students can be assigned a partner with whom to work. At the completion of the assignment, they can be asked to evaluate their partner's work based upon established criteria. Some points to consider could be: What do you think the sample shows your partner can do? What do you think your partner did well? What do you think your partner could make better?

Experiments and/or demonstrations:
Students complete an experiment or demonstration and present it through an oral or written report. Students can be evaluated on their understanding of the concept, their explanation of the scientific method, and/or their language proficiency.

Self-assessment:
Students benefit tremendously from a self-assessment because through the process of self-analysis they begin to think for themselves. Instructors need to provide guidance as well as the criteria related to success.

Student journals:
Students benefit from journals because they are useful for keeping records and for promoting an inner dialogue.

Portfolios:
A portfolios is a collection of the student's work over a period of time (report cards, creative writing, drawing, and so on) that also function as an assessment, because it

- indicates a range of competencies and skills; and
- is representative of instructional goals and academic growth.

Skill 11.2   **Identify appropriate measurement concepts (e.g., reliability, validity), test characteristics, and uses of norm-referenced and criterion-referenced assessments in evaluating ELLs**

The constructs of reliability and validity are crucial in assessing ELLs because of the high stakes involved in testing in today's schools. Decisions about schools, teachers, and students are based on these tests. A reliable assessment test for ELLs will have three attributes: validity, reliability, and practicality.

Validity: An assessment test can be considered valid only if it measures what it asserts to measure. If an ELL assessment test claims to measure oral proficiency, then the test should include a section in which instructors ask the ELL to pronounce certain words, listen to the instructor's pronunciation and determine if it is correct, and/or respond directly to the instructor's questions.

According to Diaz-Rico and Weed (1995), ". . . empirical validity is a measure of how effectively a test relates to some other known measure." There are different types of validity: predictive and concurrent (Diaz-Rico and Weed 1995). **Predictive** empirical validity is concerned with the possible outcomes of test performance, and **concurrent** empirical validity is connected with another variable for measurement. For example, if a learner shows a high English speech proficiency in class, then the instructor would have the expectation that the learner would perform well during an oral proficiency exam.

Reliability: An assessment test can be considered reliable only if similar scores result when the test is retaken. Factors such as anxiety, hunger, tiredness, and uncomfortable environmental conditions should not cause a huge fluctuation in the learner's score. Typically, if a learner earns a score of 90 percent on a test that the instructor created, then averages predict that the learner probably scored 45 percent on one half of the test and 45 percent on the other half, regardless of the structure of the test items.

Practicality: A test that proves to be both valid and reliable may unfortunately prove to be cost- or time-prohibitive. The ideal assessment test would be easy to administer and easy to grade and would include testing items similar to what the learners have experienced in class. However, when learners encounter test items such as writing journals, practicality becomes an issue. A writing journal, although an excellent method for learners to explore their critical literacy skills and track language achievement progress, can be difficult to grade due to the subjective content and may not be an accurate representation of what the learners have encountered in class.

Scoring: The scoring of ELL's performance on state-mandated norm-referenced tests has become an issue, in part, because of the NCLB Act of 2001. ELL children are the disproportionately low-income sector and more likely to attend schools with fewer resources (Neill 2005). Therefore, they frequently begin behind (and rarely catch up) in the adequate yearly progress (AYP) reports the act requires. In previous years, schools did not worry very much about this. However, high-stakes testing has made this a very important issue in schools, school districts, and states that are competing for federal funds under the revised Elementary and Secondary Education Act (ESEA).

See also Skill 9.1.

Skill 11.3   **Use a variety of instruments (e.g., portfolios, checklists, rubrics, anecdotal records) to assess students as they perform authentic tasks (e.g., real-world, contextualized)**

The following are examples of alternative assessments that offer options for an instructor.

Conferencing:
This assessment tool allows the instructor to evaluate a student's progress or decline. Students also learn techniques for self-evaluation.

Oral interviews:
Teachers can use oral interviews to evaluate the language the students are using or their ability to provide content information when asked questions—both of which have implications for further instructional planning. Oral interviews also may indicate problem areas that need addressing.

Teacher observation:

During this type of assessment, the instructor observes the student's behavior during an activity alone or within a group. Before doing the observation, the instructor may want to create a numerical scale to rate desired outcomes.

Documentation:

Documentation is similar to teacher observation. However, documentation tends to take place over a longer period of time.

Story or text retelling:

Students respond orally and can be assessed on how well they describe events in the story or text, on their response to the story, and/or on their language proficiency.

Rubrics:

Rubrics are pre-established guidelines for students and teachers that spell out the criteria on which students' work will be evaluated. Different levels could be: Beginning, Developing, Accomplished, and Exemplary. Rubrics are used to develop communication between the teacher and the student because they can pinpoint where the student needs to improve.

Checklists:

Checklists are designed to help the teacher monitor and evaluate different indicators of performance. Indicators are documentable or measureable pieces of information regarding some learning objective.

See also Skill 11.1.

Skill 11.4   Identify appropriate test-taking skills and strategies needed by ELLs

ELLs must be taught the language of tests and test-taking skills. Tests often contain predictable phrases and formats that learners need to know, such as: 'What is the main idea of the paragraph?', 'Give two facts to support your reason', and so on. When provided with specifics, ELLs can focus on the test and not be intimidated by the test format and unfamiliar terminology.

See also Skill 9.1.

Skill 11.5   Determine appropriate modifications of classroom tests, including test items and tasks, for ELLs at varying English proficiency levels

The goal in every classroom is for Limited English Proficiency (LEP) students to learn the basic content areas (math, science, social studies, and so on). To accomplish this goal, LEP students must learn an academic language, which takes from five to seven years to acquire (Cummins 1993–2003), because LEP students typically encounter issues with vocabulary when being instructed in the content areas.

When checking for understanding, the instructor should do the following:

- Ask the learners to clarify the first, second, and continuing steps of a process.
- Ask a "who," "what," "when," "where," or "whose" question.
- Ask silly questions.
- Ask for clarification from the learner.
- Emphasize that making mistakes and being corrected is a basic tenet of any learning process but especially learning a language.
- Focus on what a learner is trying to communicate rather than on how correct the communication is.
- When the error interferes with understanding, restate the question or sentence correctly.

In addition to the preceding strategies, remember the following: always announce and write down the objectives for a particular unit; use handwriting that is readable; develop consistency through daily routines; list step-by-step instructions; and use blended instructional approaches whenever possible. All these approaches will make the ELL more likely to perform better when evaluated because he or she will know the formats and routines of assessment.

GLOSSARY OF ABBREVIATIONS AND ACRONYMS

AAPPL (ACTFL Assessment of Performance toward Proficiency in Languages): a language proficiency test maintained by the American Council for the Teaching of Foreign Languages (ACTFL)

ACE (asking, cooperating, empathizing): basic social strategies for second language acquisition

BICS (basic interpersonal communication skills): a type of language proficiency that ELLs must acquire to function informally in social situations

CALLA (Cognitive Academic Language Learning Approach): a teaching method that helps ELLs gain proficiency in their target language by focusing on academic subject matter

CALP (cognitive academic language proficiency): a type of language proficiency that is more demanding than BICS

CBI (content-based instruction): teaching that uses core academic subjects, such as mathematics, social studies, or science, as the foundation for ESL lessons

CUP (Common Underlying Proficiency): skills, ideas, and concepts that ELLs can transfer from their first language to their English learning

DREAM (Development, Relief, and Education of Alien Minors): proposed federal act that would provide alien minors the opportunity to earn conditional permanent residency

ELD (English Language Development): model of English language immersion education

ELL (English language learner): student who is learning the English language in addition to his or her native language

ELPS (English Language Proficiency Standards): standards and levels used to determine ELLs' English language proficiency

ESL (English as a Second Language): study of the English language by speakers whose native language is not English

ESOL (English for Speakers of Other Languages): alternative form of the term *ESL*

IC (instructional conversations): interactive form of initiation and feedback

L1 (first language): an ELL's native language

L2 (second language): an ELL's second language

LAD (Language Acquisition Device): special biological brain mechanism with which all humans are born, as explained in the theory of Noam Chomsky

LEA (Language Experience Approach): teaching approach in which students create a narrative that provides content for instruction

LEP (Limited English Proficient): a government-defined term describing ELLs with restricted access to learning

LET (lowering anxiety, encouragement, taking emotional temperature): basic affective strategies for second language acquisition

LULAC (League of United Latin American Citizens): founded in 1929, the oldest and most widely respected Hispanic civil rights organization in the United States of America. LULAC was created at a time in U.S. history when Hispanics were denied basic civil and human rights, despite contributions to American society. The founders of LULAC created an organization that empowers its members to create and develop opportunities where they are needed most. http://lulac.org/about/history/

NCLB (No Child Left Behind): federal act of 2001 that established requirements that school districts must meet to continue to receive federal funds

PPP (Presentation, Practice, Production): model in which teachers present small amounts of language to help ELLs acquire communication skills

PRAC (practicing, receiving, analyzing, creating): basic cognitive strategies for second language acquisition

PTO (parent-teacher organization): a school organization or association (sometimes called PTA) that consists of parents, teachers, and staff members

SVO (subject, verb, object): common sentence structure in the English language

TOEFL (Test of English as a Foreign Language): language proficiency test used as an entrance exam to U.S. colleges and universities

TPR (Total Physical Response): technique using verbal commands and physical gestures to increase the ELL's oral production

BIBLIOGRAPHY

Arreaga-Mayer, C. 1998. "Increasing Active Student Responding and Improving Academic Performance through Classwide Peer Tutoring." *Intervention in School and Clinic* 34: 89–94.

Atkinson, R., and D. Hansen. 1966–1967. "Computer-assisted Instruction in Initial Reading: The Stanford Project." *Reading Research Quarterly* 2: 5–26.

Bailey, K. 1983. "Competitiveness and Anxiety in Adult Second Language Learning: Looking at and through the Diary Studies." In H. W. Seliger and M. H. Long (eds.), *Classroom-Oriented Research in Second Language Acquisition.* Rowley, MA: Newbury House.

Berko Gleason, J. 1993. *The Development of Language.* 3rd ed. New York: Macmillan.

Bermudez, A., and D. Palumbo. 1994. "Bridging the Gap between Literature and Technology: Hypermedia as a Learning Tool for Limited English Proficient Students." *Journal of Educational Issues of Language Minority Students* 14: 165–184.

Bialystok, E., ed. 1991. *Language Processing in Bilingual Children.* Cambridge: CUP.

Blanton, L. L. 1992. "A Holistic Approach to College ESL: Integrating Language and Content." *ELT Journal* 46: 285–293.

Bransford, J. E., and M. K. Johnson. 1972. "Contextual Prerequisites for Understanding: Some Investigations of Comprehension and Recall." *Journal of Verbal Learning and Verbal Behavior* 11: 717–726.

Breen, M., and C. N. Candlin. (1980). "The Essentials of a Communicative Curriculum in Language Teaching." *Applied Linguistics* 1 (2): 89–112.

Brown, A. 2008. "Gesture Viewpoint in Japanese and English: Cross-Linguistic Interactions between Two Languages in One Speaker." *Gesture* 8 (2): 256–276.

Brown, A. L., J. D. Bransford, R. A. Ferrara, and J. C. Campione. 1983. "Learning, Remembering, and Understanding." In J. H. Flavell and E. M. Markman (eds.), *Handbook of Child Psychology.* Vol. 3. New York: Wiley, pp. 77–166.

Burgess, Y., and S. Trinidad. 1997. "Young Children and Computers: Debating the Issues." *Australian Educational Computing* 12 (1): 16–21.

Candlin, C. 1987. In R. Batstone. 1994. *Grammar.* Oxford: OUP.

Carrell, P. L., and J. C. Eisterhold. 1983. "Schema Theory and ESL Reading Pedagogy." *TESOL Quarterly* 17 (4): 553–573.

Cassidy, S. 2004. "Learning Styles: An Overview of Theories, Models, and Measures." *Educational Psychology* 24: 419–444.

Cazden, C. 1983. "Adult Assistance to Language Development: Scaffolds, Models, and Direct Instruction." *Developing Literature*. Delaware: International Reading Association.

Celce-Murcia, M., ed. 1991. *Teaching English as a Second or Foreign Language*. 2nd ed. Boston: Heinle and Heinle.

Center for Applied Linguistics. SIOP. http://www.cal.org/siop/

Chamot, A. U., and J. M. O'Malley. 1994. *The CALLA Handbook: Implementing the Cognitive Academic Language Learning Approach*. Reading, MA: Addison-Wesley.

Chapman, D. W., and C. W. Snyder, Jr. 2000. *Can High Stakes National Testing Improve Instruction? Reexamining Conventional Wisdom*. Elsevier Science Ltd.

Collier, V. P. 1989. "How Long? A Synthesis of Research on Academic Achievement in Second Language." *TESOL Quarterly* 23: 509–31.

Collier, V. P. 1992. "A Synthesis of Studies Examining Long-Term Language Minority Student Data on Academic Achievement." *Bilingual Research Journal* 16 (1–2): 187–212.

Collier, V. P. 1995. "Acquiring a Second Language for School." *Directions in Language & Education* 1 (4): 1–10.

Collier, V. P. 1998. *Promoting Academic Success for ESL Students*. New Jersey Teachers of English to Speakers of Other Languages: Bilingual Educators.

Cooperstein, S., and E. Kocevar-Weidinger. 2004. "Beyond Active Learning: A Constructivist Approach to Learning." *Reference Services Review* 82 (2): 141–148.

Crandall, J. 1992. "Content-Centered Instruction in the United States." *Annual Review of Applied Linguistics* 13: 111–126.

Crandall, J., J. Jaramillo, J. Olsen, et al. 2002. "Using Cognitive Strategies to Develop English Language and Literature." Washington, DC: ERIC Clearinghouse on Languages and Linguistics, Center for Applied Linguistics.

Cummins, J. 1981. *Bilingualism and Minority Language Children*. Toronto: Institute for Studies in Education.

Cummins, J. 1984. *Bilingualism and Special Education: Issues in Assessment and Pedagogy*. San Diego: College Hill Press.

Cummins, J. 1998. "Rossell and Baker: Their Case for the Effectiveness of Bilingual Education." *Journal of Pedagogy Pluralism and Practice* 3 (1), Fall.

Cummins, J., and M. Genzuk. 1991. "Analysis of Final Report Longitudinal Study of Structured English Immersion Strategy, Early-Exit and Late-Exit Transitional Bilingual Education Programs for Language-minority Students." *California Association for Bilingual Education Newsletter* 13.

Day, R. R., and J. Bamford. 1998. *Extensive Reading in the Second Language Classroom*. Cambridge: CUP.

Díaz-Rico, L. T. 2008. *Strategies for Teaching English Learners*. 2nd ed. Boston: Pearson.

Díaz-Rico, L. T., and K. Z. Weed. 2013. *Cross-Cultural, Language, and Academic Development Handbook: A Complete K–12 Reference Guide.* 5th ed.. Needham Heights, MA: Allyn and Bacon.

Dulay, H., and M. Burt. 1974. "You Can't Learn without Goofing." In J. Richards (ed.), *Error Analysis: Perspectives on Second Language Acquisition.* New York: Longman.

Echevarria, J. 1995. "Interactive Reading Instruction: A Comparison of Proximal and Distal Effects of Instructional Conversations." *Exceptional Children* 61(6): 536–552.

Ellis, R. 1994. *The Study of Second Language Acquisition.* Oxford: OUP.

ELPS: English Language Proficiency Standards. Education Service Center, Region 4 (ESC4), 2009. 2 Jan. 2014. <www.esc4.net/docs/122-ELPS.pdf>

Enright, D. S. 1991. "Supporting Children's English Language Development in Grade Level and Language Classrooms." (In Celce-Murcia, M. 1991).

Finocchiaro, M., and C. Brumfit. 1983. *The Functional-notional Approach: From Theory to Practice.* New York: Oxford University Press.

Florida Public Virtual Schools. FDOE. Virtual education. http://www.fldoe.org/default.asp

Garcia, E. 2001. *Student Cultural Diversity: Understanding and Meeting the Challenge.* 3rd ed. Boston: Houghton Mifflin.

Gardner, H. 1999. *Intelligence Reframed: Multiple Intelligences for the 21st Century.* New York: Basic Books.

Gardner, R., and W. Lambert. 1972. *Attitudes and Motivation in Second Language Learning.* Cambridge, MA: Newbury House.

Genesee, F. 1987. *Learning through Two Languages: Studies of Immersion and Bilingual Education.* Cambridge, MA: Newbury House.

Genesee, F., ed. 1994. *Educating Second Language Children: The Whole Child, the Whole Curriculum, the Whole Community.* Cambridge: CUP.

Genesee, F., et al. 2006. *Conclusions and Future Directions.* New York: Cambridge University Press.

Goodman, K. S. 1986. *What's Whole about Whole Language? A Parent/Teacher Guide to Children's Learning.* Portsmouth, NH: Heinemann.

Grellet, F. 1981. *Developing Reading Skills.* Cambridge: CUP.

Graves, M., et al. 2012. *Teaching Vocabulary to English Languages Learners.* New York: Teachers College Press.

Hartley, K., and L. D. Bendixen. 2001. "Educational Research in the Internet Age: Examining the Role of Individual Characteristics." *Educational Researcher* 30 (9).

Hoven, D. 1992. "CALL in a Language Learning Environment." *CAELL Journal* 3 (2): 19–27.

Hoven, D. 1996. "Communicating and Interacting: An Exploration of the Changing Roles of Media in CALL/CMC." *Calico Journal* 23 (2): 233–256.

Howatt, A. (1984). *A History of English Language Teaching*. Oxford: Oxford University Press.

Hughes, A. 1989. *Testing for Language Teachers*. New York: Cambridge University Press.

Johns, K. M., and N. M. Tórrez. "Helping ESL Learners Succeed." *Phi Delta Kappa* 484: 7–49.

Kramsch, C. 1998. *Language and Culture*. Oxford: OUP.

Krashen, S. 1982. *Principles and Practice in Second Language Acquisition*. Oxford: Pergamon Press.

Krashen, S., and T. Terrell. 1983. *The Natural Approach: Language Acquisition in the Classroom*. Oxford: Pergamon Press.

Language Assessment Scales Oral (LAS-O) – English. http://ericae.net/eac/eac0132.htm

Larsen-Freeman, D. 1997. "Chaos/Complexity Science and Second Language Acquisition." *Applied Linguistics* 18 (2): 141–165.

McDonough, J., and S. Shaw. 1993. *Materials and Methods in ELT: A Teacher's Guide.* London: Blackwell.

McKeon, D. 1987. *Different Types of ESL Programs*. Washington, DC: ERIC Clearinghouse on Language and Linguistics.

McLaughlin, B. 1990. "The Development of Bilingualism: Myth and Reality." In A. Barona and E. Garcia (eds.), *Children at Risk: Poverty, Minority Status, and Other Issues in Educational Equity*. Washington, DC: National Association of School Psychologists, pp. 65–76.

Mohan, B., and W. A. Lo. 1985. "Academic Writing and Chinese Students' Transfer and Developmental Factors." *TESOL Quarterly* 19: 515–534.

Moll, L. C. 1998. "Turning to the World: Bilingualism, Literacy and the Cultural Mediation of Thinking." *National Reading Conference Yearbook* 47: 59–75.

Murray, G., and S. Kouritzen. 1997. "Re-thinking Second Language Instruction, Autonomy and Technology: A Manifesto." *System* 25 (2): 185–196.

Ninio, A., and J. Bruner. 1988. "The Achievements and Antecedents of Labelling." In M. Franklin and S. Barten (eds.), *Child Language: A Reader*. New York: Oxford University Press.

Nunan, D. 1989. *Designing Tasks for the Communicative Classroom*. Cambridge: CUP.

Omaggio Hadley, A. (1993). *Teaching Language in Context* (2nd ed.), Chapter 3: On teaching a language – Principles and priorities in methodology (pp. 73–124). Boston: Heinle & Heinle.

O'Malley, J. M. and L. V. Pierce. 1996. *Authentic Assessment for English Language Learners: Practical Approaches for Teachers*. Boston: Longman/Addison Wesley.

Orange County Public Schools. Parent Leadership Resources. https://www.ocps.net/cs/multilingual/parents/Pages/PLCInstitute.aspx

Padrón, Y. N., and H. C. Waxman. 1996. "Improving the Teaching and Learning of English Language Learners through Instructional Technology." *International Journal of Instructional Media* 23 (4): 341–354.

Paris, S. G., and B. K. Lindauer. 1976. "The Role of Inference in Children's Comprehension and Memory." *Cognitive Psychology* 8: 217–227.

Peregoy, S. F., and O. F. Boyle. 2008. *Reading, Writing, and Learning in ESL*. 5th ed. Boston: Pearson.

Perera, K. 1993. "Standard English in Attainment of Target One." *Language Matters*. Centre for Primary Education 3: 10.

Plyler v. Doe 457 U.S. 202. 1982. http://supreme.justia.com/cases/federal/us/457/202/case.html

Prabhu, N. S. 1987. *Second Language Pedagogy: A Perspective*. London: OUP.

Pressley, M. 2002. "What Should Reading Comprehension Instruction Be the Instruction of?" In M. Kamil, P. Mosenthal, P. D. Pearson, and R. Barr (eds.), *Handbook of Reading Research*. Vol. 3. Mahwah, NJ: Erlbaum, pp. 545–561.

"Proficiency Level Descriptors." *Telpas Resources*. Texas Education Agency. 19 Dec. 2013. 2 Jan. 2014. <http://www.tea.state.tx.us/student.assessment/ell/telpas/>

Reid, J. "The Learning Style Preferences of ESL Students." *TESOL Quarterly* 21 (1): 86–103.

Reilly, T. 1998. "ESL through Content Area Instruction." ERIC No. ED296572. May 1988. 12 Feb. 2014. http://www.eric.ed.gov.

Rennie, J. 1993. "ESL and Bilingual Program Models." *Eric Digest*. Sept. 1993. 12 Feb. 2014. <http://www.cal.org/resources/Digest/rennie01.html>.

Reyhner, J. 1997. *Teaching Indigenous Languages*. Compilation of papers from a symposium at Northern Arizona University Department of Modern Languages. 25.2. Flagstaff, AZ.

Richards, J. 1971. "A Non-contrastive Approach to Error Analysis." *English Language Teaching* 25: 205–219.

Richards, Platt, and Weber. 1985. Quoted by Ellis, R." The Evaluation of Communicative Tasks in Tomlinson, B (ed.)" *Materials Development in Language Teaching*. Cambridge: CUP. 1998.

Riding, R. J., and I. Cheema. 1991. "Cognitive Styles: An Overview and Integration." *Educational Psychology,* 11 (3, 4): 193–215.

Saunders, W. M., and C. Goldenberg. 1999. "Effects of Instructional Conversations and Literature Logs on Limited- and Fluent-English-Proficient Students' Story Comprehension and Thematic Understanding." *Elementary School Journal* 99 (4): 277–301.

Saville-Troike, M. 1986. "Anthropological Considerations in the Study of Communication." In *Nature of Communication Disorders in Culturally and Linguistically Diverse Populations.* San Diego: College Hill Press.

Schmidt, R., and S. Frota. 1986. "Developing Basic Conversational Ability in a Second Language: A Case Study of an Adult Learner in Portuguese." In R. R. Day (ed.), *Talking to Learn: Conversation in Second Language Acquisition.* Rowley, MA: Newbury House, pp. 237–326.

Schumm, J. S., ed. 2006. *Reading Assessment and Instruction for All Learners.* New York: Guilford Press.

Selinker, L. 1972. "Interlanguage." *International Review of Applied Linguistics in Language Teaching* 10 (3): 209.

Selinker, L. 1992. *Rediscovering Interlanguage.* London: Longman.

Sinclair, J., and M. Coulthard. 1975. *Towards an Analysis of Discourse.* Oxford: OUP, pp. 93–94.

Teachers of English to Speakers of Other Languages. 1997. *ESL Standards for Pre-K–12 Students.* Alexandria, VA: TESOL.

Thomas, W. P., and V. P. Collier. 1995. *Language Minority Student Achievement and Program Effectiveness.* Manuscript in preparation. (In Collier, V. P. 1995.)

Thompson, R. 1996. "Assimilation." *Encyclopedia of Social and Cultural Anthropology.* Vol. 1. New York: Henry Holt and Co.

Trudgill, P. 1984. *Applied Sociolinguistics.* London: Academic Press.

Ur, P. 1996. *A Course in Language Teaching.* Cambridge: CUP.

Van Ek, J. A. 1990. *The Threshold Level in a European Unit-Credit System for Modern Language Learning by Adults.* Strasbourg: Council of Europe.

Volusia County Schools. PLC - Parent Leadership Council. http://myvolusiaschools.org/esol/Pages/PLC-Parent-Leadership-Council.aspx

Vygotsky, L. S. 1986. *Thought and Language.* Cambridge, MA: MIT Press.

Vygotsky, L. S. 2006. *Mind in Society.* Cambridge, MA: Harvard University Press.

Watson, S. 2011. Learning Disability Checklist. 12 Feb. 2014. <http://specialed.about.com/cs/learningdisabled/a/LDstrengthweak.htm >

Webster, J. "Inclusion—What is Inclusion? Federal Law Requires Students with Disabilities Learn with Typical Peers." http://specialed.about.com/od/integration/a/Inclusion-What-Is-Inclusion.htm

Wilkins, D. A. 1976. *Notional Syllabus*. Oxford: Oxford University Press.

Zainuddin, H., et al. 2007. *Fundamentals of Teaching English to Speakers of Other Languages in K–12 Mainstream Classrooms.* 2nd ed. Dubuque: Kendall/Hunt.

Zwiers, J. 2008. *Building Academic Language: Essential Practices for Content Classrooms, Grades 5–12*. San Francisco: Jossey-Bass.

Zwiers, J., and M. Crawford. 2011. *Academic Conversations: Classroom Talk That Fosters Critical Thinking and Content Understandings.* Portland, ME: Stenhouse Publishers.

SAMPLE TEST

1. **What is the best program for teaching ELLs?**
    (Average) (Skill 1.1)

    A. error analysis

    B. grammar-based ESL

    C. structured English immersion

    D. no single program

2. **How can teachers, students and ELLs learn about other cultures?**
    (Easy) (Skill 1.1)

    A. by studying the grammar of the language

    B. by critically reviewing the history of the culture one is studying

    C. by studying the history and art forms

    D. by reading about it in news magazines

3. **When teaching ELLs about time, how could the teacher teach the students about timed tests if speed is not important in the native culture?**
    (Easy) (Skill 1.2)

    A. give timed practice tests

    B. allow the ELLs to finish their work at their own pace

    C. discuss the consequences of not finishing on time

    D. praise students who complete their tasks on time

4. **What cultural taboo might cause some children refuse to eat a pepperoni and cheese pizza?**
    (Average) (Skill 1.2)

    A. It goes against their dietary laws.

    B. The pizza is cold.

    C. Pizza should be eaten with a knife and fork.

    D. Classmates have told them not to eat it because it is unhealthy.

5. **Which one of the following is NOT considered a stage of acculturation?**
    (Average) (Skill 1.3)

    A. The Honeymoon Stage

    B. The Hostility Stage

    C. The Exit Stage

    D. The Humor Stage

6. **Which one of the following is a result of assimilation?**
    (Easy) (Skill 1.3)

    A. Recent immigrants learn the language of the desired culture perfectly, but it takes a long time.

    B. Immigrants achieve a high socioeconomic level.

    C. Immigrants move away from the intense geographic concentration of their fellow immigrants.

    D. Immigrants become dependent on social welfare.

7. **Which one of the following resources would NOT have research documents for graduate courses?**
    (Easy) (Skill 1.4)

    A. Center for Applied Linguistics

    B. TESOL Journal

    C. ERIC

    D. webquests

8. **On which one of the following websites would an ELL student be able to find practice exercises?**
    (Average) (Skill 1.4)

    A. http://www.nabe.org

    B. www.esl.about.com

    C. http://www2.ed.gov/about/offices/list/oela/index.html

    D. http://www.ed.gov

9. **How can teachers demonstrate cultural sensitivity when using "teacher talk" in the classroom?** *(Easy) (Skill 1.5)*

   A. increase the wait time for answers

   B. encourage the students to "speak up"

   C. ask only questions to which students must respond with a "formulaic" answer

   D. move on quickly to other students when the student called upon doesn't answer

10. **What is the main reason that oral discussions of reading materials is important in the ESOL classroom?** *(Average) (Skill 1.5)*

    A. Teachers can call on anyone since they all read the same book.

    B. Students are able to negotiate meaning.

    C. Students can question the culture mentioned in the reading text.

    D. Students can participate in a non-threatening classroom activity.

11. **The Parent Leadership Councils (PLCs) are a direct result of which of the following judicial decisions or legislation?** *(Easy) (Skill 1.6)*

    A. Lau v. Nichols

    B. Title III, NCLB Act

    C. Proposition 227

    D. The Florida Consent Decree of 1990

12. **According to the Pew Research Institute, approximately what percentage of the U.S. population growth will be attributed to immigrants arriving in the U.S. between 2005 and 2050?** *(Average) (Skill 1.7)*

    A. 22%

    B. 42%

    C. 62%

    D. 82%

13. **Which one is NOT a benefit of embracing multiculturalism?** *(Easy) (Skill 1.7)*

    A. Reduce isolation

    B. Promote healthy intercultural relations

    C. Less condemning of cultures associated with terrorist attacks

    D. Increased globalization

14. **What is meant when we say "Language is interdependent?"** *(Easy) (Skill 2.1)*

    A. Language can be changed to other modalities.

    B. Language is in continual change.

    C. Language uses arbitrary symbols.

    D. Language is an integrated structure.

15. **What is the result of insufficient practice in listening to a sound new to the ELL?** *(Average) (Skill 2.2)*

    A. inadequate vocabulary

    B. frustration for the learner

    C. heavy accent

    D. poor reading skills

16. **When the voice rises at the end of a question, which of the following items is being used to determine meaning?** *(Easy) (Skill 2.2)*

    A. stress

    B. pitch

    C. articulation

    D. phonemes

17. **In the word in<u>access</u>ible, the underlined part is the** *(Easy) (Skill 2.3)*

    A. prefix

    B. compound

    C. root

    D. suffix

18. **"You can't have your cake and eat it too" is an example of** *(Easy) (Skill 2.4)*

    A. a line of poetry

    B. an idiom

    C. a famous saying

    D. hyperbole

19. **When parents ask children if they have brushed their teeth and know that they haven't, they are using which of the following language devices?** *(Easy) (Skill 2.5)*

    A. pragmatics

    B. hyperbole

    C. metaphor

    D. semantics

20. **The study of word order which creates meaning is the study of...**
(Easy) (Skill 2.6)

   A. pragmatics

   B. semantics

   C. syntax

   D. register

21. **ELLs who learn a language through thought processes use which of the following skills?**
(Easy) (Skill 2.6)

   A. social

   B. cognitive

   C. psycholinguistic

   D. verbal

22. **One characteristic of discourse is:**
(Average) (Skill 2.7)

   A. It shapes the way we organize our thoughts.

   B. It is lengthy.

   C. It is culturally independent.

   D. It is the same in all disciplines.

23. **What is 'empty language'?**
(Easy) (Skill 2.7)

   A. perfunctory speech with little meaning

   B. language with some content

   C. CALPs

   D. pattern less speech

24. **What are CUPs?**
(Easy) (Skill 2.7)

   A. Common Underlying Proficiency

   B. Common Unit Proficiencies

   C. Cognitive Underlying Paradigms

   D. Cognitive Unit Proficiencies

25. **Which one of the following is NOT a reason people change their register?**
(Easy) (Skill 2.8)

   A. formality of the situation

   B. attitude toward a topic

   C. relationship to other speakers

   D. degree of an ELL's assimilation

26. **Which one of the following is a reason NOT to try to eliminate variations in English by ELLs?**
(Easy) (Skill 2.8)

   A. There is only one standard English.

   B. All students need to speak the same way to avoid an inferiority complex among the ELLs.

   C. It can create hostility.

   D. ELLs appreciate the help in perfecting their English.

27. **The translation of the English word "cargo" to Spanish as "el cargo" is an example of which of the following?**
(Average) (Skill 2.9)

   A. genre

   B. false cognate

   C. related

   D. cognate

28. **Which researcher is associated with the LAD?**
(Easy) (Skill 3.1)

   A. Piaget

   B. Vygotsky

   C. Krashen

   D. Chomsky

29. **According to theories concerning 'intentionality', what is the best way to promote language in children?**
(Average) (Skill 3.1)

   A. engaging them in conversation

   B. letting them watch children's TV programs

   C. correcting their errors in gentle ways

   D. truly listening to them

30. **Researchers who focus on the mistakes language learners make are studying which one of the following?**
(Easy) (Skill 3.1)

   A. interlanguage

   B. developmental patterns

   C. error analysis

   D. language acquisition

31. **According to Krashen's theory of second language acquisition, which of the following concerns how learners best learn new material?**
(Easy) (Skill 3.1)

   A. The Acquisition-Learning Hypothesis

   B. The Monitor Hypothesis

   C. The Input Hypothesis

   D. The Affective Filter Hypothesis

32. Which stage is the language learner in when he or she knows about 3,000 receptive words and communicates using short phrases and sentences?
(Average) (Skill 3.2)

   A. silent period

   B. simplified speech

   C. experimental speech

   D. lexical chunks

33. In which immersion education model is the student taken out of the regular classroom for English language instruction?
(Average) (Skill 3.3)

   A. grammar-based ESL

   B. communication-based ESL

   C. submersion with primary language support

   D. structured English immersion

34. Free and Appropriate Public Education and Least Restrictive Environment are two important concepts resulting from which piece of legislation?
(Average) (Skill 3.3)

   A. Title III, NCLB Act

   B. Education of all Handicapped Children Act

   C. Florida Consent Decree

   D. Lau v. Nichols

35. Which one of the following is NOT required for a language learner to achieve fluency?
(Easy) (Skill 3.4)

   A. study in the foreign language country

   B. time

   C. practice

   D. comprehensible input

36. In homes where both parents are bilingual, what language practice is recommended for raising bilingual children?
(Average) (Skill 3.5)

   A. speaking only the language of the country in which the language learner resides

   B. speaking both languages to the child as early as possible

   C. using only the language that culturally most important

   D. speaking one language when socializing and the other language when studying

37. Children from 6 to 12 continue to develop which of the following skills in their native language?
(Easy) (Skill 3.6)

   A. pragmatics in oral language

   B. vocabulary

   C. semantics

   D. all of the above

38. According to Ogbu's studies, which of the following is NOT a characteristic of caste-like minorities?
(Average) (Skill 3.7)

   A. They were exploited.

   B. They held low-paying jobs.

   C. They valued education as a way to escape.

   D. Many hold undesirable jobs.

39. Which of the following factors increases the L1's chances of acquiring L2?
(Average) (Skill 3.7)

   A. little mutual respect between the L1 and L2 groups

   B. incompatibility between L1 and L2

   C. negative attitudes

   D. both the L1 and L2 groups want assimilation for the L1 group

40. Which of the following terms applies when a second language learner desires to learn a language because of an interest in the culture being studied?
(Average) (Skill 3.8)

   A. instrumental motivation

   B. self-esteem

   C. integrative motivation

   D. attitude

41. How do children learn BICS?
(Easy) (Skill 3.9)

   A. by studying the grammar of the language

   B. naturally in their social environment

   C. from studying ESL activities in the classroom

   D. in special classes

42. **According to Cummins, which level of difficulty is a person practicing when they are writing a research report?**
(Average) (Skill 3.9)

A. Level 1: Cognitively undemanding / context-embedded

B. Level 2: Cognitively undemanding / context-reduced

C. Level 3: Cognitively demanding / context-embedded

D. Level 4: Cognitively demanding / context-reduced

43. **By using which of the following can teachers in upper grades reduce the difficulty of tasks for students still learning CALPs?**
(Average) (Skill 3.9)

A. by using realia and demonstrations

B. by offering different books and encyclopedias on the subject

C. by repeating the lesson until the ELL grasps it Punctuation

D. by allowing the ELL to stay after school for special tutoring

44. **According to Selinker's theory of interlanguage, which of the following is NOT a learner strategy?**
(Average) (Skill 3.10)

A. overgeneralization

B. simplification

C. L1 Interference

D. L2 interference

45. **When a student says, "Me go eat", which of the following strategies is the learner using?**
(Easy) (Skill 3.10)

A. overgeneralization

B. simplification

C. L1 Interference

D. fossilization

46. **Which of the following has research shown to be a valid learning tool?**
(Easy) (Skill 3.10)

A. correcting oral grammar mistakes

B. correcting written grammar mistakes

C. correcting semantic errors

D. correcting beginning learners only

47. **According to Wilkins, which of the following is a function?** *(Easy) (Skill 3.11)*

    A. I did my homework early so I could watch Facebook.

    B. I am sorry.

    C. Let me do that for you.

    D. bright blue sky

48. **Which of the following statements about reading is false?** *(Easy) (Skill 4.1)*

    A. Children must learn to read a second time in English.

    B. Teachers can build upon the L1 literacy of the ELL.

    C. It is necessary to thoroughly evaluate the L1 reading ability to best initiate L2 reading instruction.

    D. Reading teachers can build upon the language experiences of an ELL's native or heritage language.

49. **According to Peregoy and Boyle, a child whose writing contains a somewhat sequenced text with several sentences is at which of the following levels in their writing?** *(Easy) (Skill 4.2)*

    A. Beginning Level

    B. Intermediate Level

    C. Advanced Level

    D. Superior Level

50. **According to Krashen, which of the following falls under Stage 4 (the last stage) of morpheme acquisition?** *(Average) (Skill 4.3)*

    A. auxiliary verbs

    B. irregular past tense verbs

    C. copula

    D. third-person singular

51. **Older students are able to progress more rapidly in language learning because of which of the following?** *(Easy) (Skill 4.4)*

    A. They are smarter.

    B. They know how to use their life experiences to understand L2.

    C. Teachers enjoy working with older learners more than with children.

    D. Older learners dedicate more time to studying.

52. **Which one of the following scaffolding criteria is unnecessary for readers who are becoming proficient?**
(Average) (Skill 4.5)

   A. meaningful communication found in whole texts

   B. language and discourse patterns that are repetitive

   C. a model of the text to be produced

   D. reading materials below grade level

53. **Which of the following is NOT a reason to use L1 instruction with an ELL when available?**
(Easy) (Skill 4.5)

   A. It will hinder their acquisition of L2.

   B. L1 lowers the affective filter.

   C. L1 clarifies misunderstandings in L2.

   D. L1 can be used to explain the similarities and differences between the two languages.

54. **What is the basic principle of CALLA?**
(Average) (Skill 5.1)

   A. It requires ELLs to respond to commands with actions.

   B. This approach states that being accurate is not as important as the learner enjoying the process.

   C. It is used to transition ESOL-driven language arts program to a 'mainstream' language arts program.

   D. It consists of eight interrelated components that help prepare lessons for ELLs.

55. **According to the work of Winitz, language learners used which one of the following techniques in learning a language?**
(Easy) (Skill 5.2)

   A. visual aids/clues, gestures

   B. touching one of four pictures to indicate a correct response

   C. using audio cassettes and a book with illustrations

   D. practiced structures using notions/functions

56. When students are asked to create a graph using information found in a reading passage, they are using techniques developed by which researcher?
(Average) (Skill 5.2)

A. Terrell and Krashen

B. Lewis

C. Gattegno

D. Prabhu

57. Which of the following language approaches emphasizes the use of the actual language being used in the content areas as language for learning?
(Average) (Skill 5.3)

A. CALLA

B. SIOP

C. TPR

D. The Natural Approach

58. Which one of the following is the main activity in Language Experience Approach?
(Easy) (Skill 5.4)

A. physical activity

B. opinion-gap activities

C. individual responsibility for own learning

D. creation of a narrative with content for instruction

59. Which one of the following was not provided for in Lau v. Nichols?
(Average) (Skill 5.5)

A. funding

B. improved educational conditions for LEP students

C. equal access to any academic program

D. Lau Remedies

60. What one of the following was NOT discovered by the American Institute for Research when they studied the results of Proposition 227?
(Average) (Skill 5.5)

A. Students had about the same results as before Proposition 227 was implemented.

B. Students had a chance of being reclassified as language proficient of more than 36%.

C. The performance gap remained constant over the five years of the study.

D. The methods recommended by Proposition 227 had no significant impact on the success of ELLs.

61. **The Consent Decree of 1990 provided for which of the following?** *(Easy) (Skill 5.5)*

    A. LEP students receive a generalized plan of education.

    B. LEP students will have access to programs designed for language learners.

    C. LEP students will have access to certified instructors.

    D. LEP students may not receive diplomas until five years of schooling are achieved.

62. **Under the Equal Access to Appropriate Programming section of the Consent Decree, which of the following is provided to students?** *(Easy) (Skill 5.6)*

    A. Students receive an education in basic technical skills.

    B. Students receive instruction in basic subject areas aligned with their proficiency levels in English.

    C. Students can request instruction in their heritage language.

    D. Students do not receive programs to support their academic needs, only those which support their language needs.

63. **Programs are monitored by which of the following departments to ensure compliance with the Consent Decree?** *(Easy) (Skill 5.6)*

    A. Office of Academic Achievement through Language Achievement (AALA)

    B. LULAC

    C. Office of LEP Supervision

    D. U. S. Department of Education

64. **Which of the following services are NOT available to ELLs?** *(Easy) (Skill 5.6)*

    A. extended day care

    B. math instruction

    C. early childhood programs

    D. all of the above

65. **Which one of the following is the best way to present a listening activity to ELLs?**
(Easy) (Skill 6.1)

   A. State the purpose of the activity.

   B. Introduce the passage by saying, "You are going to hear…".

   C. Ask students answer questions about the activity at the conclusion of the exercise.

   D. Request students close their books and listen carefully to the audio.

66. **Which one of the following is a benefit of group work for ELLs?**
(Average) (Skill 6.2)

   A. They are able to discuss the work in their native language.

   B. They lose their autonomy by subjecting their opinions to the group.

   C. Group work usually produces simpler language than when students work alone.

   D. The language produced is not really authentic.

67. **The science teacher gave each student in a small group a paper with one or two facts about growing plants. The students had to organize the information into a sequenced step-by-step set of instructions, and then summarize the activity. Which of the following activities was she practicing?**
(Average) (Skill 6.3)

   A. roundtable

   B. information gap activity

   C. interview

   D. writing headlines

68. **When the instructor asks the ELLs to identify the word endings in a text, she is emphasizing which of the following?**
(Easy) (Skill 6.4)

   A. syntactic clues

   B. semantic clues

   C. phonemic clues

   D. graphemic clues

69. **Which one of the following techniques is NOT beneficial to students learning to read in a foreign language?**
(Easy) (Skill 6.4)

   A. creating personal dictionaries

   B. journal writing

   C. encouraging students to read for their own pleasure in their native language

   D. studying vocabulary lists

70. **Identify the characteristic of a poor reader.**
    (Easy) (Skill 6.4)

    A. grasps chunks of language

    B. unable to self-monitor

    C. maintains comprehension

    D. decodes automatically

71. **Which type of graph would help students activate prior knowledge before commencing on a new topic?**
    (Easy) (Skill 6.4)

    A. a bar graph

    B. a flow chart

    C. a KWL chart

    D. a Venn diagram

72. **What is the main purpose of quick-writes and learning logs?**
    (Average) (Skill 6.5)

    A. to allow the student to summarize their thoughts

    B. to give students a chance to explore their ideas

    C. to give ungraded writing practice

    D. to let students have a quiet moment in the classroom

73. **Which of the following is the most beneficial to students while learning to write an essay about their favorite sports figure using U. S. conventions?**
    (Average) (Skill 6.5)

    A. studying the textbook instructions

    B. following the teacher's guidelines

    C. encouraging students to read essays or biographies of their hero

    D. thoroughly analyzing a sample essay

74. **In order to develop an essay evaluating the importance of a judicial law, which one of the following would be the best way to develop the essay?**
    (Easy) (Skill 6.6)

    A. spatial order

    B. chronological order

    C. logical order

    D. order of importance

75. The instructor asked students to request menus from different restaurants where they like to eat. They then practiced ordering from the menus. In what type of learning activity were they engaged?
(Easy) (Skill 6.7)

   A. task-based learning

   B. CBI

   C. SIOP

   D. a jigsaw activity

76. Which of the following would be an appropriate strategy to use in an elementary school theme-based unit on dinosaurs?
(Easy) (Skill 6.8)

   A. use of functions/notions for communication

   B. whole language approach

   C. traditional teaching of the content areas

   D. TPR

77. Which of the following sets of contains one item not mentioned in Enright's seven key instructional criteria for designing and conducting instruction to support an ELL's language and literacy development?
(Average) (Skill 6.9)

   A. collaboration, support, variety, integration

   B. collaboration, purpose, student interest, support

   C. purpose, support, previous knowledge, language level

   D. purpose, student interest, support, integration

78. The ESOL instructor wants to incorporate previous knowledge into her unit on mythology before starting the unit. Which of the following would be a good way to do this?
(Easy) (Skill 6.9)

   A. comparing folktales from native cultures with the unit's tales

   B. researching the origins of mythology

   C. comparing two mythological characters as the unit develops

   D. reviewing the unit before a test

79. **Which of the following is NOT a collaborative activity that would benefit ELLs in their language learning experiences?**
(Easy) (Skill 6.9)

   A. student-teacher dialog journals

   B. interacting with people outside the classroom

   C. discussion groups

   D. watching an assigned TV program followed by an oral report

80. **The ESOL teacher who explains to her Spanish-speaking students that the Spanish suffix 'cion" is the same as the English suffix 'tion' is helping her students develop their vocabulary by recognizing which of the following?**
(Easy) (Skill 7.1)

   A. morphemes

   B. true cognates

   C. copulas

   D. hyperbole

81. **Which one of the following is NOT a criticism of CALL?**
(Easy) (Skill 7.3)

   A. computer-generated feedback for measuring learners' speaking ability is inaccurate

   B. learners who are computer illiterate were disadvantaged

   C. testing was limited by the lack of content

   D. most students enjoy working with computers or handheld devices

82. **Identify the most important advantage of CMC.**
(Easy) (Skill 7.3)

   A. It is socially friendly.

   B. It requires students to prepare to use it.

   C. There is little control over the language used.

   D. Students quickly go off topic.

83. **What is one advantage of CMC according to Kroonenberg?**
(Easy) (Skill 7.3)

   A. Emails provide realistic communication between real people.

   B. Chat-rooms are potentially dangerous to ELLs.

   C. The topics discussed are not relevant.

   D. Since the ELLs are just learning a new language, the language used is not realistic.

84. **Which of the following statements about Florida's virtual school is true?**
(Easy) (Skill 7.3)

   A. The program is run by individual schools.

   B. Students use these programs as an alternative to attending regular classes.

   C. The program is small but growing in recognition.

   D. The programs are inferior to classroom instruction.

85. **Which of the following public resources can supplement the resources of immigrant ELLs who may need help with research for homework assignments?**
(Easy) (Skill 7.4)

   A. the YMCA and YWCA

   B. parks

   C. afterschool programs

   D. the public library

86. **What is one of the main provisions of the Consent Decree?**
(Easy) (Skill 8.1)

   A. regular classroom teachers are used

   B. only one approach or model be used

   C. instruction always be understandable for ELLs

   D. native language may not be used in the classroom

87. In preparing for a group work activity, the teacher requested the students arrange their desks in groups of four facing each other. What was the main purpose of the rearrangement of the desks?
(Easy) (Skill 8.2)

   A. to eliminate the need for supervision

   B. to ensure individual results

   C. to ensure group interaction

   D. to lower the volume during the activity

88. Why do ELLs frequently do well in mathematics?
(Easy) (Skill 8.3)

   A. They understand word problems well.

   B. Mathematical symbols are the same or similar in native cultures.

   C. Children naturally like math.

   D. The use of manipulatives make math fun.

89. When the ESOL instructor wants her eighth grade students to practice their numbers, which one of the following would provide an enjoyable activity?
(Easy) (Skill 8.4)

   A. practicing phone numbers

   B. learning the multiplication tables

   C. the song No More Monkeys Jumping on the Bed

   D. discuss the superstitions surrounding numbers

90. The students have been assigned an essay writing assignment. When she questions an ELL saying, 'What is your main idea?' or 'Do you have three supporting details for that statement'? What scaffolding technique is the instructor using?
(Easy) (Skill 8.5)

   A. shared

   B. modeling

   C. guided

   D. independent

91. **Selinker defined fossilization as which of the following?**
(Easy) (Skill 8.6)

A. the inability to hear incorrect speech

B. the inability to reproduce certain sounds

C. the lack of interest in improving certain speech or written patterns

D. a level of high competency

92. **In order to tackle the fossilization errors of her ELLs, which of the following suggestions would be the most appropriate?**
(Easy) (Skill 8.6)

A. ignore the errors in the written work and tackle the oral errors

B. ignore the errors in speech and work on the written papers

C. tape the oral errors to create mini-lessons

D. reteach the pertinent unit

93. **Which of the following standard practices would probably disconcert a student not familiar with U.S. standardized testing?**
(Easy) (Skill 9.1)

A. being permitted to only work on one section of the test at a time

B. inability to use a calculator on a math test

C. a proctor who is not the classroom teacher

D. inability to use a translating dictionary on a vocabulary test

94. **Which testing bias would occur if a reading passage contained the statement 'The early bird catches the worm'?**
(Easy) (Skill 9.1)

A. attitudinal bias

B. test bias

C. norming bias

D. translation bias

95. Which of the following techniques can an instructor use to reduce test anxiety?
(Easy) (Skill 9.1)

   A. have the test administered by an impartial proctor

   B. be flexible with time limitations

   C. identify unusual content beforehand

   D. give practice tests frequently

96. Which one of the following area does the SOLOM test NOT cover?
(Average) (Skill 9.2)

   A. comprehension

   B. fluency

   C. vocabulary

   D. reading

97. Which one of the following accommodations is permitted under T1 for ELLs with at least one year in the schooling system?
(Average) (Skill 9.3)

   A. reading of the vocabulary parts of the test

   B. allowing additional time

   C. explanation of the test question

   D. reading of the comprehension parts of the test

98. Which of the following methods is the most reliable method to date for determining if an ELL is exhibiting learning difficulties?
(Average) (Skill 9.4)

   A. testing for language proficiency

   B. testing for grade level performance

   C. observation and interpretation

   D. use of standardized testing instruments

99. Which one of the following is an example of a language similarities second language development and language disorders?
(Average) (Skill 9.5)

   A. experience difficulties in following directions

   B. stuttering

   C. unable to produce certain sounds

   D. have issues with pitch

100. **Which one of the following is an example of a language learner experiencing problems with speech motor skills?**
(Average) (Skill 9.5)

   A. mispronounces phonemes

   B. creating speech that is not understandable to others

   C. confusing certain grammatical structures

   D. lacks advanced vocabulary

101. **What cultural factor might cause word problems to be difficult for an ELL?**
(Easy) (Skill 9.6)

   A. because of the simplicity of the language

   B. because of the economic context in which it is placed

   C. because of vision problems

   D. because of poor reading skills

102. **What might be a reason for a non-gifted ELL to act out in class?**
(Easy) (Skill 9.6)

   A. The ELL is suffering from PTSD.

   B. The ELL is familiar with US norms regarding behavior.

   C. the instructor's scaffolding is appropriate

   D. The ELL's hearing is normal.

103. **In evaluating a student for referral to ESE, which of the following would NOT be a sign of L2 difficulties in some students?**
(Average) (Skill 9.6)

   A. expressive difficulties

   B. behavioral differences

   C. reading difficulties

   D. difficulties controlling emotions

104. **Which piece of legislation listed below is NOT part of the Consent Decree compliance mandates?**
(Average) (Skill 10.1)

   A. Requirements of Plyler v. Doe

   B. Section 504 of the Rehabilitation Act of 1973

   C. Equal Education Opportunities Act of 1974

   D. Title I (1965)

105. **The NCLB act of 2002, specifically focused on which of the following groups of children?**
(Easy) (Skill 10.1)

A. students aiming for college admission

B. children overlooked by the educational system

C. children of veterans

D. children of single mothers

106. **According to the NCLB Act of 2002, which of the following statements is false?**
(Easy) (Skill 10.1)

A. Standardized testing can be deferred one-time for one year, on a case-by-case basis for students receiving ESL services.

B. Puerto Rican students may be exempt from taking standardized testing in English even if they have attended U.S. schools for 3 years.

C. LEP students do not have to be included in all academic testing administered to other students.

D. Tests are to be administered in the language most likely to provide accurate data of the LEP's academic achievement and performance.

107. **Which of the following tests would be administered by a school to determine how well an ELL understands the rules of punctuation?**
(Average) (Skill 10.2)

A. a language placement test

B. a language achievement test

C. a language proficiency test

D. a language diagnostic test

108. **The TOEFL is which of the following types of tests?**
(Easy) (Skill 10.2)

A. proficiency

B. achievement

C. diagnostic

D. placement

109. **Why must language testing be done cautiously?**
(Easy) (Skill 10.2)

   A. Tests are unreliable because they are not well prepared.

   B. Tests don't measure achievement.

   C. Language tests measure only a small portion of possible language dimensions.

   D. Language tests measure the wrong variables.

110. **In addition to Parent Leadership Councils (PLC), how does Florida inform parents about issues concerning their children?**
(Easy) (Skill 10.3)

   A. through webpages

   B. issuing policy statements to the legislature

   C. sending home notices

   D. calling up parents

111. **What is the role of the instructor when students are asked to provide self-assessment?**
(Easy) (Skill 11.1)

   A. to provide the formats

   B. to encourage honesty

   C. to allow exaggeration

   D. to provide the criteria

112. **Which one of the following is NOT a benefit of journals?**
(Easy) (Skill 11.1)

   A. ELLs gain additional writing practice.

   B. Journals provide the teacher with an additional grade for each student.

   C. Journals are useful for keeping records.

   D. Journals are helpful in promoting an inner dialogue for the student.

113. **In the language of testing, what is the definition of validity?**
(Easy) (Skill 11.2)

   A. a test that measures correct language

   B. a test that measures test items accurately

   C. accurate scoring of test items

   D. a test which measures what it claims to measure

114. **When an ELL demonstrates good oral skills in class, which of the following terms would an ESOL instructor expect to apply an oral proficiency test of the ELL?**
(Average) (Skill 11.2)

A. concurrent validity

B. reliability

C. predictive validity

D. practicality

115. **What is the value of alternative assessments?**
(Easy) (Skill 11.3)

A. They are contextualized.

B. They are more structured.

C. Teacher observations are more accurate.

D. Teachers know more about how to test their own students.

116. **When evaluating a student during a story or text exercise, which of the following would a teacher be observing?**
(Easy) (Skill 11.3)

A. the students reaction to the material

B. the interpretation of the material

C. response to the illustrations

D. written responses

117. **Why are rubrics a valuable way for ELLs' to understand their problems?**
(Average) (Skill 11.3)

A. Rubrics illustrate how the ELL compares with other students.

B. Rubrics compare the student with standardized testing.

C. Rubrics establish guidelines for a particular exercises or set of exercises.

D. Rubrics are good documentation for teachers.

118. **What is one reason for teaching phrases such as 'Identify the main idea of the paragraph' and 'Circle the word which shows that means x' before a administering a standardized test?**
(Average) (Skill 11.4)

A. teaches chunks of language

B. illustrates idioms for students

C. raises the affective filter

D. permits familiarity with the language of tests

119. **Which of the following techniques would be inappropriate to use when quickly checking for understanding of a reading passage?**
(Average) (Skill 11.5)

A. give a timed quiz

B. ask a silly question

C. ask the student to retell the passage

D. focus on what is being communicated not the grammar

120. **When language errors interfere with understanding, what technique could an instructor use to correct the ELL without drawing attention to the error?**
(Easy) (Skill 11.5)

A. explain why the language is incorrect

B. restate the question or sentence correctly

C. say ' I don't understand.'

D. make the learner restate his or her question or statement

ANSWER KEY

1.	D	41.	B	81.	D
2.	C	42.	D	82.	A
3.	A	43.	A	83.	A
4.	A	44.	D	84.	B
5.	C	45.	B	85.	D
6.	C	46.	C	86.	C
7.	D	47.	D	87.	C
8.	B	48.	A	88.	B
9.	A	49.	B	89.	A
10.	B	50.	D	90.	C
11.	D	51.	B	91.	C
12.	D	52.	D	92.	B
13.	C	53.	A	93.	A
14.	D	54.	C	94.	D
15.	C	55.	C	95.	D
16.	B	56.	D	96.	D
17.	C	57.	A	97.	B
18.	B	58.	D	98.	C
19.	A	59.	A	99.	A
20.	C	60.	B	100.	B
21.	B	61.	C	101.	B
22.	A	62.	B	102.	A
23.	A	63.	A	103.	D
24.	A	64.	D	104.	D
25.	D	65.	B	105.	B
26.	C	66.	A	106.	C
27.	B	67.	D	107.	B
28.	D	68.	A	108.	A
29.	D	69.	D	109.	C
30.	C	70.	B	110.	A
31.	C	71.	C	111.	D
32.	D	72.	C	112.	B
33.	D	73.	C	113.	D
34.	B	74.	D	114.	A
35.	A	75.	A	115.	A
36.	B	76.	B	116.	A
37.	D	77.	C	117.	C
38.	C	78.	A	118.	D
39.	D	79.	D	119.	A
40.	C	80.	B	120.	B

RATIONALES

1. **What is the best program for teaching ELLs?**
   (Average) (Skill 1.1)

   A. error analysis
   B. grammar-based ESL
   C. structured English immersion
   D. no single program

Answer: D. no single program
Despite years of research by many different researchers, there is still no single approach or program that serves all needs.

2. **How can teachers, students and ELLs learn about other cultures?**
   (Easy) (Skill 1.1)

   A. by studying the grammar of the language
   B. by critically reviewing the history of the culture one is studying
   C. by studying the history and art forms
   D. by reading about it in news magazines

Answer: C. by studying the history and art forms
The best way to learn about the culture of another country is to study the history (from impartial sources) and studying the various art forms of the other culture.

3. **When teaching ELLs about time, how could the teacher teach the students about timed tests if speed is not important in the native culture?**
   (Easy) (Skill 1.2)

   A. give timed practice tests
   B. allow the ELLs to finish their work at their own pace
   C. discuss the consequences of not finishing on time
   D. praise students who complete their tasks on time

Answer: A. give timed practice tests
The best way to change a cultural practice such as staying on target and finishing a task within the allotted time is to give practice tests. Simply discussing the consequences or praising students who complete their tasks on time will probably not have much effect on ELLs.

4. **What cultural taboo might cause some children refuse to eat a pepperoni and cheese pizza?**
(Average) (Skill 1.2)

   A. It goes against their dietary laws.
   B. The pizza is cold.
   C. Pizza should be eaten with a knife and fork.
   D. Classmates have told them not to eat it because it is unhealthy.

Answer: A. It goes against their dietary laws.
B, C and D are all possible reasons a child might not eat a pizza. However, answer A is a cultural one. In some cultures, it is a violation of religious laws to mix dairy and meat products in the same dish or by using the same utensils.

5. **Which one of the following is NOT considered a stage of acculturation?**
(Average) (Skill 1.3)

   A. The Honeymoon Stage
   B. The Hostility Stage
   C. The Exit Stage
   D. The Humor Stage

Answer: C. The Exit Stage
A, B, and C are three of the stages of acculturation. (The Home Stage is the fourth.) Therefore, the Exit Stage is the correct answer.

6. **Which one of the following is a result of assimilation?**
(Easy) (Skill 1.3)

   A. Recent immigrants learn the language of the desired culture perfectly, but it takes a long time.
   B. Immigrants achieve a high socioeconomic level.
   C. Immigrants move away from the intense geographic concentration of their fellow immigrants.
   D. Immigrants become dependent on social welfare.

Answer: C. Immigrants move away from the intense geographic concentration of their fellow immigrants.
A, B, and D are three possibilities, but are not true of most immigrants. Immigrants do tend to seek better living conditions by moving away from enclaves of fellow immigrants as they become more familiar with the culture of the country in which they now reside.

7. **Which one of the following resources would NOT have research documents for graduate courses?**
   (Easy) (Skill 1.4)

   A. Center for Applied Linguistics
   B. TESOL Journal
   C. ERIC
   D. webquests

Answer: D. webquests
A researcher should be able to find research papers in all of the resources mentioned except WebQuest. WebQuest helps teachers build thematic units for classroom use.

8. **On which one of the following websites would an ELL student be able to find practice exercises?**
   (Average) (Skill 1.4)

   A. http://www.nabe.org
   B. www.esl.about.com
   C. http://www2.ed.gov/about/offices/list/oela/index.html
   D. http://www.ed.gov

Answer: B. www.esl.about.com
Answer A is the website for the National Association for Bilingual Education. Answer C is The website for The U. S. Dept. of Education, Office of Language Acquisition, Language Enhancement and Academic Achievement for Limited English Proficient Students. Answer D is the website of the U.S. Dept. of Education. Only Answer B is a website designed for students as well as teachers.

9. **How can teachers demonstrate cultural sensitivity when using "teacher talk" in the classroom?**
   (Easy) (Skill 1.5)

   A. increase the wait time for answers
   B. encourage the students to "speak up"
   C. ask only questions to which students must respond with a "formulaic" answer
   D. move on quickly to other students when the student called upon doesn't answer

Answer: A. increase the wait time for answers
Only answer A demonstrates cultural sensitivity. The other answers do not encourage participation of ELLs.

10. What is the main reason that oral discussions of reading materials is important in the ESOL classroom?
(Average) (Skill 1.5)

    A. Teachers can call on anyone since they all read the same book.
    B. Students are able to negotiate meaning.
    C. Students can question the culture mentioned in the reading text.
    D. Students can participate in a non-threatening classroom activity.

Answer: B. Students are able to negotiate meaning.
Answer A is false since many students don't read their assignment. Answer C is a possibility, but this would probably not be the objective of an ESOL class. Answer D is false for many students since speaking orally in the classroom is a threatening activity. Only Answer B would be a valid language objective for ELLs.

11. The Parent Leadership Councils (PLCs) are a direct result of which of the following judicial decisions or legislation?
(Easy) (Skill 1.6)

    A. Lau v. Nichols
    B. Title III, NCLB Act
    C. Proposition 227
    D. The Florida Consent Decree of 1990

Answer: D. The Florida Consent Decree of 1990
The correct answer is D.

12. According to the Pew Research Institute, approximately what percentage of the U.S. population growth will be attributed to immigrants arriving in the U.S. between 2005 and 2050?
(Average) (Skill 1.7)

    A. 22%
    B. 42%
    C. 62%
    D. 82%

Answer: D. 82%
The correct answer is D.

13. Which one is NOT a benefit of embracing multiculturalism?
(Easy) (Skill 1.7)

   A. Reduce isolation.
   B. Promote healthy intercultural relations.
   C. Less condemning of cultures associated with terrorist attacks.
   D. Increased globalization.

Answer: C. Less condemning of cultures associated with terrorist attacks.
Answers A,B, and D are all certain benefits. Answer C is unfortunately the opposite; 9/11 has caused major setbacks with more condemning and stereotyping of the Middle Eastern and Muslim cultures.

14. What is meant when we say "Language is interdependent?"
(Easy) (Skill 2.1)

   A. Language can be changed to other modalities.
   B. Language is in continual change.
   C. Language uses arbitrary symbols.
   D. Language is an integrated structure.

Answer: D. Language is an integrated structure.
Answers A, B, and C are all properties of language as is the interdependence of language. The definition of language interdependence is answer D--language is an integrated structure.

15. What is the result of insufficient practice in listening to a sound new to the ELL?
(Average) (Skill 2.2)

   A. inadequate vocabulary
   B. frustration for the learner
   C. heavy accent
   D. poor reading skills

Answer: C. heavy accent
ELLs need to hear a sound and try to imitate it, especially if it is a new sound to them. The lack of practice in both areas will result in a heavy accent otherwise.

16. When the voice rises at the end of a question, which of the following items is being used to determine meaning?
(Easy) (Skill 2.2)

    A. stress
    B. pitch
    C. articulation
    D. phonemes

Answer: B. pitch
Stress can modify the meaning of a word or a sentence, but in this case we are talking about the voice using a rising tone at the end of a sentence to ask a question. Articulation refers to units of sound. Phonemes are the smallest unit of sound that influences meaning.

17. In the word inaccessible, the underlined part is the
(Easy) (Skill 2.3)

    A. prefix
    B. compound
    C. root
    D. suffix

Answer: C. root
Answer C is the correct answer.

18. "You can't have your cake and eat it too" is an example of ...
(Easy) (Skill 2.4)

    A. a line of poetry
    B. an idiom
    C. a famous saying
    D. hyperbole

Answer: B. an idiom
The correct answer is B.

19. When parents ask children if they have brushed their teeth and know that they haven't, they are using which of the following language devices?
(Easy) (Skill 2.5)

    A. pragmatics
    B. hyperbole
    C. metaphor
    D. semantics

Answer: A. pragmatics
Hyperbole is exaggerated speech. Metaphors make indirect comparisons. Semantics is the study of the meaning of words and word combinations. The correct answer is A pragmatics where an implication to brush your teeth is made to the child.

20. The study of word order which creates meaning is the study of...
(Easy) (Skill 2.6)

    A. pragmatics
    B. semantics
    C. syntax
    D. register

Answer: C. syntax
Pragmatics is the study of how language is used to imply meaning. Semantics is the study of the meaning of words. Register is the degree of language formality used in different social situations. The correct answer is C syntax.

21. ELLs who learn a language through thought processes use which of the following skills?
(Easy) (Skill 2.6)

    A. social
    B. cognitive
    C. psycholinguistic
    D. verbal

Answer: B. cognitive
By using their thought processes more, they are considered to learn through cognitive processes.

22. One characteristic of discourse is ...
(Average) (Skill 2.7)

A. It shapes the way we organize our thoughts.
B. It is lengthy.
C. It is culturally independent.
D. It is the same in all disciplines.

Answer: A. It shapes the way we organize our thoughts.
Discourse can be short, and it varies considerably in the different disciplines. Discourse is culturally dependent, and it shapes the way we think. Therefore, A is the correct answer.

23. What is 'empty language'?
(Easy) (Skill 2.7)

A. perfunctory speech with little meaning
B. language with some content
C. CALPs
D. pattern less speech

Answer: A. perfunctory speech with little meaning
Perfunctory speech is speech that follows set patterns for opening and closing a conversation politely, and is the correct answer.

24. What are CUPs?
(Easy) (Skill 2.7)

A. Common Underlying Proficiency
B. Common Unit Proficiencies
C. Cognitive Underlying Paradigms
D. Cognitive Unit Proficiencies

Answer: A. Common Underlying Proficiency
Common Underlying Proficiencies are the language skills, ideas, and concepts that can be transferred from L1 to L2. Answer A is the correct choice.

25. Which one of the following is NOT a reason people change their register?
(Easy) (Skill 2.8)

    A. formality of the situation
    B. attitude toward a topic
    C. relationship to other speakers
    D. degree of an ELL's assimilation

Answer: D. degree of an ELL's assimilation
A, B, and C are all reasons we change our register. The ELL probably has little control over the register he or she chooses. Therefore, the degree of assimilation is the correct answer.

26. Which one of the following is a reason NOT to try to eliminate variations in English by ELLs?
(Easy) (Skill 2.8)

    A. There is only one standard English.
    B. All students need to speak the same way to avoid an inferiority complex among the ELLs.
    C. It can create hostility.
    D. ELLs appreciate the help in perfecting their English.

Answer: C. It can create hostility.
Over compulsive correction of the ELL's language efforts will probably do more harm than good. In today's world, there are more nonnative speakers of English than native speakers. Language variations are the norm, not the exception. Therefore, C is the correct answer.

27. The translation of the English word "cargo" to Spanish as "el cargo" is an example of which of the following?
(Average) (Skill 2.9)

    A. genre
    B. false cognate
    C. related
    D. cognate

Answer: B. false cognate
Genre refers to a type of literature. Cognates and related words are synonyms derived from the same source. In this case, cargo in English means freight or "la carga". The Spanish, 'el cargo', in Spanish means job or post. Hence, this is an example of a false cognate or words that may appear to be similar but are not.

28. Which researcher is associated with the LAD?
(Easy) (Skill 3.1)

A. Piaget
B. Vygotsky
C. Krashen
D. Chomsky

Answer: D. Chomsky

Piaget theorized that language is a reflection of thought. Vygotsky believed that language is first a social communication which progresses to language and cognition. Krashen's work revolved around his theory of second language acquisition. Chomsky believed that humans are born with a special biological brain mechanism called the Language Acquisition Device or LAD. D is the correct answer.

29. According to theories concerning 'intentionality', what is the best way to promote language in children?
(Average) (Skill 3.1)

A. engaging them in conversation
B. letting them watch children's TV programs
C. correcting their errors in gentle ways
D. truly listening to them

Answer: D. truly listening to them

According to these theorists, the best way to promote language in young children is to truly listen to them.

30. Researchers who focus on the mistakes language learners make are studying which one of the following?
(Easy) (Skill 3.1)

A. interlanguage
B. developmental patterns
C. error analysis
D. language acquisition

Answer: C. error analysis

Interlanguage is the language that a learner develops as he or she progresses from L1 to L2. Developmental patterns concern the order in which specific language features are acquired. Language acquisition refers to Krashen's distinction between acquiring a language subconsciously while learning a language requires study. Error analysis concerns analyzing the errors committed by a learner (frequently, this is studied in written work) and helping them overcome these errors.

31. According to Krashen's theory of second language acquisition, which of the following concerns how learners best learn new material?
(Easy) (Skill 3.1)

    A. The Acquisition-Learning Hypothesis
    B. The Monitor Hypothesis
    C. The Input Hypothesis
    D. The Affective Filter Hypothesis

Answer: C. the Input Hypothesis
The Acquisition-Learning Hypothesis concerns the distinction between acquisition (acquiring a language naturally) and learning (studying) a language. The Monitor Hypothesis states that a learner monitors his or her language to eliminate mistakes. The Affective Filter Hypothesis believes we learn better in pleasant, relaxed circumstances. The Input Hypothesis states a person learns best when the language level is just above what the learner actually knows.

32. Which stage is the language learner in when he or she knows about 3,000 receptive words and communicates using short phrases and sentences?
(Average) (Skill 3.2)

    A. silent period
    B. simplified speech
    C. experimental speech
    D. lexical chunks

Answer: D. lexical chunks
In the silent period, the learner knows about 500 words. In the experimental or simplified speech stage, the learner has developed a level of fluency and can make semantic and grammatical generalizations. The correct answer is D, the lexical chunk stage.

33. In which immersion education model is the student taken out of the regular classroom for English language instruction?
(Average) (Skill 3.3)

    A. grammar-based ESL
    B. communication-based ESL
    C. submersion with primary language support
    D. structured English immersion

Answer: D. structured English immersion
In grammar-based ESL, emphasis is on the language itself or usage. In communication-based ESL, the emphasis is on communicating or use of the language. In submersion with primary language support, the goal is English proficiency and students review English language content in their primary language. D is the correct answer--structured English immersion.

34. Free and Appropriate Public Education and Least Restrictive Environment are two important concepts resulting from which piece of legislation?
(Average) (Skill 3.3)

A. Title III, NCLB Act
B. Education of all Handicapped Children Act
C. Florida Consent Decree
D. Lau v. Nichols

Answer: B. Education of all Handicapped Children Act
The correct answer is B.

35. Which one of the following is NOT required for a language learner to achieve fluency?
(Easy) (Skill 3.4)

A. study in the foreign language country
B. time
C. practice
D. comprehensible input

Answer: A. study in the foreign language country
Time, practice and comprehensible input are all required for language proficiency. Study in the country of a language is not.

36. In homes where both parents are bilingual, what language practice is recommended for raising bilingual children?
(Average) (Skill 3.5)

A. speaking only the language of the country in which the language learner resides
B. speaking both languages to the child as early as possible
C. using only the language that culturally most important
D. speaking one language when socializing and the other language when studying

Answer: B. speaking both languages to the child as early as possible
While parents are free to choose the model they wish, experts recommend using both language with the child as early as possible.

37. Children from 6 to 12 continue to develop which of the following skills in their native language?
(Easy) (Skill 3.6)

    A. pragmatics of oral language
    B. vocabulary
    C. semantics
    D. All of the above

Answer: D. All of the above
Children learn vocabulary, semantics and the pragmatics of oral language in their first language.

38. According to Ogbu's studies, which of the following is NOT a characteristic of caste-like minorities?
(Average) (Skill 3.7)

    A. They were exploited.
    B. They held low-paying jobs.
    C. They valued education as a way to escape.
    D. Many hold undesirable jobs.

Answer: C. They valued education as a way to escape.
All are true except C. Education is seldom a goal of these immigrants.

39. Which of the following factors increases the L1's chances of acquiring L2?
(Average) (Skill 3.7)

    A. little mutual respect between the L1 and L2 groups
    B. incompatibility between L1 and L2
    C. negative attitudes
    D. both the L1 and L2 groups want assimilation for the L1 group

Answer: D. both the L1 and L2 groups want assimilation for the L1 group
A, B, and C are negative factors in assimilation of the L1 group and its ability to learn L2.

40. Which of the following terms applies when a second language learner desires to learn a language because of an interest in the culture being studied?
(Average) (Skill 3.8)

    A. instrumental motivation
    B. self-esteem
    C. integrative motivation
    D. attitude

Answer: C. integrative motivation
A, B, and D are three characteristics of the affective domain. Answer C integrative motivation is the correct term applied to this type of individual.

41. How do children learn BICS?
(Easy) (Skill 3.9)

    A. by studying the grammar of the language
    B. naturally in their social environment
    C. from studying ESL activities in the classroom
    D. in special classes

Answer: B. naturally in their social environment
BICS, basic interpersonal communication skills are acquired naturally in the environment.

42. According to Cummins, which level of difficulty is a person practicing when they are writing a research report?
(Average) (Skill 3.9)

    A. Level 1: Cognitively undemanding / context-embedded
    B. Level 2: Cognitively undemanding / context-reduced
    C. Level 3: Cognitively demanding / context-embedded
    D. Level 4: Cognitively demanding / context-reduced

Answer: D. Level 4: Cognitively demanding / context-reduced
This task is cognitively demanding with the context-reduced because the work would come from many sources.

43. By using which of the following can teachers in upper grades reduce the difficulty of tasks for students still learning CALPs?
(Average) (Skill 3.9)

    A. by using realia and demonstrations
    B. by offering different books and encyclopedias on the subject
    C. by repeating the lesson until the ELL grasps it Punctuation
    D. by allowing the ELL to stay after school for special tutoring

Answer: A. by using realia and demonstrations
Teachers can use realia and demonstrations in the classroom to emphasis or illustrate the topic under discussion. To offer different books and encyclopedias on a topic is a difficult task according to Cummins' (Level 4: Cognitively demanding / context-reduced). Answers C and D are poor practice and would probably reduce motivation for most ELLs.

44. According to Selinker's theory of interlanguage, which of the following is NOT a learner strategy?
(Average) (Skill 3.10)

    A. overgeneralization
    B. simplification
    C. L1 Interference
    D. L2 interference

Answer: D. L2 interference
The correct answer is D.

45. When a student says, "Me go eat", which of the following strategies is the learner using?
(Easy) (Skill 3.10)

    A. overgeneralization
    B. simplification
    C. L1 Interference
    D. fossilization

Answer: B. simplification
In overgeneralization, the ELL would perhaps add the suffix '-ed' to all verbs. L1 interference appears when the ELL tries to use forms from L1 when the correct L2 form is unknown. With fossilization, the language learner has reached a plateau and does not try to increase his or her ability in L2. The correct answer is B. In this instance the ELL has simplified the language. It is understandable, but does not use correct grammar.

46. Which of the following has research shown to be a valid learning tool?
(Easy) (Skill 3.10)

   A. correcting oral grammar mistakes
   B.   correcting written grammar mistakes
   C. correcting semantic errors
   D. correcting beginning learners only

Answer: C. correcting semantic errors
Research has shown that A, B, and D are ineffective. Correcting semantic mistakes however leads to learning.

47. According to Wilkins, which of the following is a function?
(Easy) (Skill 3.11)

   A. I did my homework early so I could watch Facebook.
   B. I am sorry.
   C. Let me do that for you.
   D. bright blue sky

Answer: D. bright blue sky
Answer A, B, and C are all examples of different functions of a language. Notions are concepts expressed by a language. The correct answer is D.

48. Which of the following statements about reading is false?
(Easy) (Skill 4.1)

   A. Children must learn to read a second time in English.
   B. Teachers can build upon the L1 literacy of the ELL.
   C. It is necessary to thoroughly evaluate the L1 reading ability to best initiate L2 reading instruction.
   D. Reading teachers can build upon the language experiences of an ELL's native or heritage language.

Answer: A. Children must learn to read a second time in English.
Answer A is false. Children only learn to read once.

49. According to Peregoy and Boyle, a child whose writing contains a somewhat sequenced text with several sentences is at which of the following levels in their writing?
(Easy) (Skill 4.2)

    A. Beginning Level
    B. Intermediate Level
    C. Advanced Level
    D. Superior Level

Answer: B. Intermediate Level
The correct level is Intermediate. A superior level does not exist in their matrix, but was put in as a distractor.

50. According to Krashen, which of the following falls under Stage 4 (the last stage) of morpheme acquisition?
(Average) (Skill 4.3)

    A. auxiliary verbs
    B. irregular past tense verbs
    C. copula
    D. third-person singular

Answer: D. third-person singular
Auxiliary verbs are in Stage 2, the irregular past tense is in Stage 3, the copula (linking verbs) are in Stage 1. Only the Third-person singular is in Stage 4. D is the correct answer.

51. Older students are able to progress more rapidly in language learning because of which of the following?
(Easy) (Skill 4.4)

    A. They are smarter.
    B. They know how to use their life experiences to understand L2.
    C. Teachers enjoy working with older learners more than with children.
    D. Older learners dedicate more time to studying.

Answer: B. They know how to use their life experiences to understand L2.
It is not necessarily true that older learners are smarter or that all older language learners study more. Many teachers prefer working with young children. Research has shown that B older learners progress more rapidly in language learning because their life experiences help them understand the topics being discussed in the language lesson. B is the correct choice.

52. Which one of the following scaffolding criteria is unnecessary for readers who are becoming proficient?
(Average) (Skill 4.5)

    A. meaningful communication found in whole texts
    B. language and discourse patterns that are repetitive
    C. a model of the text to be produced
    D. reading materials below grade level

Answer: D. reading materials below grade level
The purpose of literacy scaffolding is to help students achieve grade level literacy with the criteria expressed in A, B, and C. Continuing to use materials below grade level would only reinforce material previously mastered. Krashen suggests materials should be at i + 1. Therefore, answer D is the correct choice.

53. Which of the following is NOT a reason to use L1 instruction with an ELL when available?
(Easy) (Skill 4.5)

    A. It will hinder their acquisition of L2.
    B. L1 lowers the affective filter.
    C. L1 clarifies misunderstandings in L2.
    D. L1 can be used to explain the similarities and differences between the two languages.

Answer: A. It will hinder their acquisition of L2.
Research has shown that Answer A is false.

54. What is the basic principle of CALLA?
(Average) (Skill 5.1)

    A. It requires ELLs to respond to commands with actions.
    B. This approach states that being accurate is not as important as the learner enjoying the process.
    C. It is used to transition ESOL-driven language arts program to a 'mainstream' language arts program.
    D. It consists of eight interrelated components that help prepare lessons for ELLs.

Answer: C. It is used to transition ESOL-driven language arts program to a 'mainstream' language arts program.
While each of the precepts mentioned is in its most basic form, Answer A refers to Total Physical Response (TPR). Answer B is a component of Krashen and Terrell's Natural Approach. Answer D refers to Sheltered Instruction Observation Protocol (SIOP). The correct choice is C.

55. According to the work of Winitz, language learners used which one of the following techniques in learning a language?
(Easy) (Skill 5.2)

    A. visual aids/clues, gestures
    B. touching one of four pictures to indicate a correct response
    C. using audio cassettes and a book with illustrations
    D. practiced structures using notions/functions

Answer: C. using audio cassettes and a book with illustrations
Answer A refers to the work of Gattagno (The Silent Way). Answer B refers to the work of Postovsky. Answer D refers to the work of Wilkins. Answer C is the correct response.

56. When students are asked to create a graph using information found in a reading passage, they are using techniques developed by which researcher?
(Average) (Skill 5.2)

    A. Terrell and Krashen
    B. Lewis
    C. Gattegno
    D. Prabhu

Answer: D. Prabhu
Terrell and Krashen worked with a natural approach to language learning. Lewis researched lexical chunks of language. Gattegno developed the Silent Way. Prabhu is the correct choice since his work focused on learning a language through meaningful tasks or activities.

57. Which of the following language approaches emphasizes the use of the actual language being used in the content areas as language for learning?
(Average) (Skill 5.3)

    A. CALLA
    B. SIOP
    C. TPR
    D. The Natural Approach

Answer: A. CALLA
Emphasis in SIOP is on teacher preparation and instructional objectives. With TPR emphasis is on active, physical response to commands. The Natural Approach emphasizes language learned in a natural way even though the researchers believed that more language could be learned in the content area classroom than when studying the language itself. The correct answer is A CALLA.

58. Which one of the following is the main activity in Language Experience Approach?
(Easy) (Skill 5.4)

A. physical activity
B. opinion-gap activities
C. individual responsibility for own learning
D. creation of a narrative with content for instruction

Answer: D. creation of a narrative with content for instruction
Answer A refers to TPR. Answer B refers to the work of Prabhu. Answer C refers to Communicative Language Teaching (CLT). D is the correct answer.

59. Which one of the following was not provided for in Lau v. Nichols?
(Average) (Skill 5.5)

A. funding
B. improved educational conditions for LEP students
C. equal access to any academic program
D. Lau Remedies

Answer: A. funding
Answer A funding was not part of the decision. Funding now comes under Title VII of ESEA.

60. What one of the following was NOT discovered by the American Institute for Research when they studied the results of Proposition 227?
(Average) (Skill 5.5)

A. Students had about the same results as before Proposition 227 was implemented.
B. Students had a chance of being reclassified as language proficient of more than 36%.
C. The performance gap remained constant over the five years of the study.
D. The methods recommended by Proposition 227 had no significant impact on the success of ELLs.

Answer: B. Students had a chance of being reclassified as language proficient of more than 36%.
Answers A, C, and D were all true findings of the study.

61. The Consent Decree of 1990 provided for which of the following?
(Easy) (Skill 5.5)

A. LEP students receive a generalized plan of education.
B. LEP students will have access to programs designed for language learners.
C. LEP students will have access to certified instructors.
D. LEP students may not receive diplomas until five years of schooling are achieved.

Answer: C. LEP students will have access to certified instructors.
The only provision for LEP students mentioned is C access to certified instructors.

62. Under the Equal Access to Appropriate Programming section of the Consent Decree, which of the following is provided to students?
(Easy) (Skill 5.6)

A. Students receive an education in basic technical skills.
B. Students receive instruction in basic subject areas aligned with their proficiency levels in English.
C. Students can request instruction in their heritage language.
D. Students do not receive programs to support their academic needs, only those which support their language needs.

Answer: B. Students receive instruction in basic subject areas aligned with their proficiency levels in English.
All statements are false except B which is a provision of the Consent Decree.

63. Programs are monitored by which of the following departments to ensure compliance with the Consent Decree?
(Easy) (Skill 5.6)

A. Office of Academic Achievement through Language Achievement (AALA)
B. LULAC
C. Office of LEP Supervision
D. U. S. Department of Education

Answer: A. Office of Academic Achievement through Language Achievement (AALA)
This office is under the supervision of the Florida Department of Education.

64. Which of the following services would be available to the parents of ELLs?
   (Easy) (Skill 5.6)

   A. extended day care
   B. math instruction
   C. early childhood programs
   D. all of the above

Answer: D. All of the above
By offering extended day care, math instruction, and early childhood programs, the DOE is fulfilling the special needs recognized under the Consent Decree.

65. Which one of the following is the best way to present a listening activity to ELLs?
   (Easy) (Skill 6.1)

   A. State the purpose of the activity.
   B. Introduce the passage by saying, "You are going to hear…".
   C. Ask students answer questions about the activity at the conclusion of the exercise.
   D. Request students close their books and listen carefully to the audio.

Answer: B. Introduce the passage by saying, "You are going to hear…".
Only Answer B sets the stage and allows students to draw upon previous knowledge while listening.

66. Which one of the following is a benefit of group work for ELLs?
   (Average) (Skill 6.2)

   A. They are able to discuss the work in their native language.
   B. They lose their autonomy by subjecting their opinions to the group.
   C. Group work usually produces simpler language than when students work alone.
   D. The language produced is not really authentic.

Answer: A. They are able to discuss the work in their native language.
Only Answer A is a true statement. Even though ELLs may speak in their heritage language, they must still negotiate meaning in English to complete the assignment, and the language produced may be more complex than when produced by individuals.

67. The science teacher gave each student in a small group a paper with one or two facts about growing plants. The students had to organize the information into a sequenced step-by-step set of instructions, and then summarize the activity. Which of the following activities was she practicing?
(Average) (Skill 6.3)

    A. roundtable
    B. information gap activity
    C. interview
    D. writing headlines

Answer: D. writing headlines
A roundtable activity asks each student to write his or her own answer to a question. The activity is an Information gap activities, but the students were asked to summarize it. This is not an interview. Writing headlines is a method of summarizing an activity and the correct answer.

68. When the instructor asks the ELLs to identify the word endings in a text, she is emphasizing which of the following?
(Easy) (Skill 6.4)

    A. syntactic clues
    B. semantic clues
    C. phonemic clues
    D. graphemic clues

Answer: A. syntactic clues
Semantic clues have to do with the meaning of a word. Phonemes and graphemes are how letters and letter combinations sound. The instructor is emphasizing syntactic clues or clues which demonstrate the meaning of a word based upon how the ending changes meaning. The correct answer is A.

69. Which one of the following techniques is NOT beneficial to students learning to read in a foreign language?
(Easy) (Skill 6.4)

    A. creating personal dictionaries
    B. journal writing
    C. encouraging students to read for their own pleasure in their native language
    D. studying vocabulary lists

Answer: D. studying vocabulary lists
Only Answer D would be a poor practice. All other options are recommended by reading specialists.

70. Identify the characteristic of a poor reader.
   (Easy) (Skill 6.4)

   A. grasps chunks of language
   B. unable to self-monitor
   C. maintains comprehension
   D. decodes automatically

Answer: B. unable to self-monitor
Only Answer B is a sign of a poor reader. All other answers are signs of fluent readers.

71. Which type of graph would help students activate prior knowledge before commencing on a new topic?
   (Easy) (Skill 6.4)

   A. a bar graph
   B. a flow chart
   C. a KWL chart
   D. a Venn diagram

Answer: C. a KWL chart
Answers a, B, and D are all useful in classroom learning situations. However, only the What we know, What we want to know and What we have learned (KWL) chart is specifically designed to help students visualize what they and what they need to know. Answer C is the correct answer.

72. What is the main purpose of quick-writes and learning logs?
   (Average) (Skill 6.5)

   A. to allow the student to summarize their thoughts
   B. to give students a chance to explore their ideas
   C. to give ungraded writing practice
   D. to let students have a quiet moment in the classroom

Answer: C. to give ungraded writing practice
While all answers have some value, the main purpose of the writing exercises is to give students ungraded writing practice.

73. Which of the following is the most beneficial to students while learning to write an essay about their favorite sports figure using U. S. conventions?
(Average) (Skill 6.5)

    A. studying the textbook instructions
    B. following the teacher's guidelines
    C. encouraging students to read essays or biographies of their hero
    D. thoroughly analyzing a sample essay

Answer: C. encouraging students to read essays or biographies of their hero
All of the answers are beneficial to students. However, researchers constantly remind us of the value of reading to further other language skills. Answer C is the correct answer.

74. In order to develop an essay evaluating the importance of a judicial law, which one of the following would be the best way to develop the essay?
(Easy) (Skill 6.6)

    A. spatial order
    B. chronological order
    C. logical order
    D. order of importance

Answer: D. order of importance
Essays of evaluation are typically developed using order of importance. D is the correct answer.

75. The instructor asked students to request menus from different restaurants where they like to eat. They then practiced ordering from the menus. In what type of learning activity were they engaged?
(Easy) (Skill 6.7)

    A. task-based learning
    B. CBI
    C. SIOP
    D. a jigsaw activity

Answer: A. task-based learning
Answer B refers to content-based instruction. Answer C is sheltered instruction observation protocol. Answer D requires large sections of text divided between a group. The correct answer is A.

76. Which of the following would be an appropriate strategy to use in an elementary school theme-based unit on dinosaurs?
(Easy) (Skill 6.8)

   A. use of functions/notions for communication
   B. whole language approach
   C. traditional teaching of the content areas
   D. TPR

Answer: B. whole language approach
The use of functions/notions for communication would probably contribute little to learning classroom content. Traditional teaching of the content leaves much to be desired when working with ELLs who may not grasp the material because of their lack of language skills. TPR is only designed for students to physically act out commands. The correct choice would be Answer B the whole language approach where students can engage in language as an integrated whole. The focus is on an integrated approach within a meaningful context. The correct choice is B.

77. Which of the following sets of contains one item not mentioned in Enright's seven key instructional criteria for designing and conducting instruction to support an ELL's language and literacy development?
(Average) (Skill 6.9)

   A. collaboration, support, variety, integration
   B. collaboration, purpose, student interest, support
   C. purpose, support, previous knowledge, language level
   D. purpose, student interest, support, integration

Answer: C. purpose, support, previous knowledge, language level
Answer is contains 'language level' which is not mentioned as a criteria by Enright.

78. The ESOL instructor wants to incorporate previous knowledge into her unit on mythology before starting the unit. Which of the following would be a good way to do this?
(Easy) (Skill 6.9)

   A. comparing folktales from native cultures with the unit's tales
   B. researching the origins of mythology
   C. comparing two mythological characters as the unit develops
   D. reviewing the unit before a test

Answer: A. comparing folktales from native cultures with the unit's tales
Only Answer A would activate previous knowledge before beginning the unit.

79. Which of the following is NOT a collaborative activity that would benefit ELLs in their language learning experiences?
(Easy) (Skill 6.9)

    A. student-teacher dialog journals
    B. interacting with people outside the classroom
    C. discussion groups
    D. watching an assigned TV program followed by an oral report

Answer: D. watching an assigned TV program followed by an oral report
Answers A, B, and C involve collaborative activities within and outside the classroom. Answer D is an individual activity and the correct answer.

80. The ESOL teacher who explains to her Spanish-speaking students that the Spanish suffix 'cion" is the same as the English suffix 'tion' is helping her students develop their vocabulary by recognizing which of the following?
(Easy) (Skill 7.1)

    A. morphemes
    B. true cognates
    C. copulas
    D. hyperbole

Answer: B. true cognates
Morphemes may be free standing such as 'chair' or derivational such as prefixes and suffixes. Copulas refer to linking verbs. Hyperbole is exaggeration. The correct answer is true cognates or Answer B.

81. Which one of the following is NOT a criticism of CALL?
(Easy) (Skill 7.3)

    A. computer-generated feedback for measuring learners' speaking ability is inaccurate
    B. learners who are computer illiterate were disadvantaged
    C. testing was limited by the lack of content
    D. most students enjoy working with computers or handheld devices

Answer: D. most students enjoy working with computers or handheld devices
All criticisms are true except D.

82. Identify the most important advantage of CMC.
(Easy) (Skill 7.3)

    A. It is socially friendly.
    B. It requires students to prepare to use it.
    C. There is little control over the language used.
    D. Students quickly go off topic.

Answer: A. It is socially friendly.
B, C and D are all possible disadvantages of CMC. The advantage of Computer-mediated Communication over CALL is that it is socially friendly. A is the correct answer.

83. What is one advantage of CMC according to Kroonenberg?
(Easy) (Skill 7.3)

    A. Emails provide realistic communication between real people.
    B. Chat-rooms are potentially dangerous to ELLs.
    C. The topics discussed are not relevant.
    D. Since the ELLs are just learning a new language, the language used is not realistic.

Answer: A. Emails provide realistic communication between real people.
B, C, and D are disadvantages of Computer-mediated Communication, not advantages. A is the correct answer.

84. Which of the following statements about Florida's virtual school is true?
(Easy) (Skill 7.3)

    A. The program is run by individual schools.
    B. Students use these programs as an alternative to attending regular classes.
    C. The program is small but growing in recognition.
    D. The programs are inferior to classroom instruction.

Answer: B. Students use these programs as an alternative to attending regular classes.
Only Answer B is a true statement.

85. Which of the following public resources can supplement the resources of immigrant ELLs who may need help with research for homework assignments?
(Easy) (Skill 7.4)

    A. the YMCA and YWCA
    B. parks
    C. afterschool programs
    D. the public library

Answer: D. the public library
The YMCA and YWCA are part of a global Christian foundation devoted to the development of body, mind and spirit. Parks would offer recreational activities, and afterschool programs generally offer afterschool homework supervision as well as recreational activities. For research, the public library would be the best choice. D is the correct answer.

86. What is one of the main provisions of the Consent Decree?
(Easy) (Skill 8.1)

    A. regular classroom teachers are used
    B. only one approach or model be used
    C. instruction always be understandable for ELLs
    D. native language may not be used in the classroom

Answer: C. instruction always be understandable for ELLs
One of the main provisions of the Consent Decree was that instruction be understandable to ELLs.

87. In preparing for a group work activity, the teacher requested the students arrange their desks in groups of four facing each other. What was the main purpose of the rearrangement of the desks?
(Easy) (Skill 8.2)

    A. to eliminate the need for supervision
    B. to ensure individual results
    C. to ensure group interaction
    D. to lower the volume during the activity

Answer: C. to ensure group interaction
Answer A suggests that having small groups will eliminate the need for supervision, and Answer D claims that the noise volume will be reduced by this arrangement. Both are doubtful. Answer B claims that individual results will be achieved by having students facing other members of the group. Again, this is doubtful. The correct answer is C where group interaction is encouraged by having students facing each other.

88. Why do ELLs frequently do well in mathematics?
(Easy) (Skill 8.3)

A. They understand word problems well.
B. Mathematical symbols are the same or similar in native cultures.
C. Children naturally like math.
D. The use of manipulatives make math fun.

Answer: B. Mathematical symbols are the same or similar in native cultures.
ELLs frequently do well in math because the symbols are the same or similar in native cultures.

89. When the ESOL instructor wants her eighth grade students to practice their numbers, which one of the following would provide an enjoyable activity?
(Easy) (Skill 8.4)

A. practicing phone numbers
B. learning the multiplication tables
C. the song No More Monkeys Jumping on the Bed
D. discuss the superstitions surrounding numbers

Answer: A. practicing phone numbers
For today's tech savvy teens, probably the most enjoyable activity would be exchanging phone numbers. (Teachers should probably emphasize using invented numbers to respect the privacy of their students.)

90. The students have been assigned an essay writing assignment. When she questions an ELL saying, 'What is your main idea?' or 'Do you have three supporting details for that statement'? What scaffolding technique is the instructor using?
(Easy) (Skill 8.5)

A. shared
B. modeling
C. guided
D. independent

Answer: C. guided
In shared scaffolding, both the instructor and student pool their knowledge. In modeling, the teacher gives examples of what is expected. With independent learners, scaffolding is no longer needed. The correct answer is C where the teacher guides the students through questions designed to elicit the expected results.

91. Selinker defined fossilization as which of the following?
(Easy) (Skill 8.6)

A. the inability to hear incorrect speech
B. the inability to reproduce certain sounds
C. the lack of interest in improving certain speech or written patterns
D. a level of high competency

Answer: C. the lack of interest in improving certain speech or written patterns
The language learner frequently does not hear errors in his or her speech even when their speech is recorded. Attempting to correct these errors usually results in little improvement. A level of moderate competency is achieved and the learner has little interest in improving. The correct answer is C.

92. In order to tackle the fossilization errors of her ELLs, which of the following suggestions would be the most appropriate?
(Easy) (Skill 8.6)

A. ignore the errors in the written work and tackle the oral errors
B. ignore the errors in speech and work on the written papers
C. tape the oral errors to create mini-lessons
D. reteach the pertinent unit

Answer: B. ignore the errors in speech and work on the written papers
The best practice is to ignore errors in speech and work on written work.

93. Which of the following standard practices would probably disconcert a student not familiar with U.S. standardized testing?
(Easy) (Skill 9.1)

A. being permitted to only work on one section of the test at a time
B. inability to use a calculator on a math test
C. a proctor who is not the classroom teacher
D. inability to use a translating dictionary on a vocabulary test

Answer: A. being permitted to only work on one section of the test at a time
Anything can upset test takers on the day of standardized testing. However, the practice of working only one section of the test at a time would probably be the most disconcerting. A is the correct answer.

94. Which testing bias would occur if a reading passage contained the statement 'The early bird catches the worm'?
(Easy) (Skill 9.1)

    A. attitudinal bias
    B. test bias
    C. norming bias
    D. translation bias

Answer: D. translation bias
Attitudinal bias refers to a negative attitude of a proctor to the test takers. Test bias or norming bias happens when ELLs or other groups are excluded from a school's population in order to obtain good norming results. Translation bias occurs when literal translation takes place. Student who are unfamiliar with the saying mentioned and tried to translate it to their native language would undoubtedly be confused. The correct answer is D.

95. Which of the following techniques can an instructor use to reduce test anxiety?
(Easy) (Skill 9.1)

    A. have the test administered by an impartial proctor
    B. be flexible with time limitations
    C. identify unusual content beforehand
    D. give practice tests frequently

Answer: D. give practice tests frequently
Tests are frequently administered by proctors who are unfamiliar to the students. This increases stress in some students. Both B and C are not permitted on standardized tests and may cause some tension if unfamiliar words are encountered. The best most instructors can do is to give practice tests to familiarize her charges with standardized testing procedures. Answer D is the correct choice.

96. Which one of the following area does the SOLOM test NOT cover?
(Average) (Skill 9.2)

    A. comprehension
    B. fluency
    C. vocabulary
    D. reading

Answer: D. reading
The Student Oral Language Observation Matrix does not include reading. The correct answer is D.

97. Which one of the following accommodations is permitted under T1 for ELLs with at least one year in the schooling system?
(Average) (Skill 9.3)

    A. reading of the vocabulary parts of the test
    B. allowing additional time
    C. explanation of the test question
    D. reading of the comprehension parts of the test

Answer: B. allowing additional time
Students may be allowed additional time. The correct answer is B.

98. Which of the following methods is the most reliable method to date for determining if an ELL is exhibiting learning difficulties?
(Average) (Skill 9.4)

    A. testing for language proficiency
    B. testing for grade level performance
    C. observation and interpretation
    D. use of standardized testing instruments

Answer: C. observation and interpretation
Testing instruments reveal much information about students. However, they do not explain the reasons why such deficiencies exist. The best method to date is observation and interpretation. The correct answer is C.

99. Which one of the following is an example of a language similarities second language development and language disorders?
(Average) (Skill 9.5)

    A. experience difficulties in following directions
    B. stuttering
    C. unable to produce certain sounds
    D. have issues with pitch

Answer: A. experience difficulties in following directions
Answers B, C, and D are examples of differences between second language development and language disorders. Answer A is an example of similarities in language disorders and second language development. A is the correct answer.

100. Which one of the following is an example of a language learner experiencing problems with speech motor skills?
(Average) (Skill 9.5)

    A. mispronounces phonemes
    B. creating speech that is not understandable to others
    C. confusing certain grammatical structures
    D. lacks advanced vocabulary

Answer: B. creating speech that is not understandable to others
Answers A, C, and D are examples of speech motor skill problems. Answer B is the correct answer. Learners who experience difficulty creating speech that others understand is a problem of speech motor skills.

101. What cultural factor might cause word problems to be difficult for an ELL?
(Easy) (Skill 9.6)

    A. because of the simplicity of the language
    B. because of the economic context in which it is placed
    C. because of vision problems
    D. because of poor reading skills

Answer: B. because of the economic context in which it is placed
Unless the Ell is bored in the classroom, simple language shouldn't be a problem. Answers C and D are problems unrelated to cultural issues. The correct answer is B. Many economic situations of the US may be unfamiliar to immigrants.

102. What might be a reason for a non-gifted ELL to act out in class?
(Easy) (Skill 9.6)

    A. The ELL is suffering from PTSD.
    B. The ELL is familiar with US norms regarding behavior.
    C. the instructor's scaffolding is appropriate
    D. The ELL's hearing is normal.

Answer: A. The ELL is suffering from PTSD.
After ruling out problems in the areas mentioned in B, C, and D, the teacher might suspect other factors. Given the political and social unrest of many countries around the world, it is possible the student is suffering from PTSD, especially if he or she comes from a country where they were forced to flee. The correct answer is A

103. In evaluating a student for referral to ESE, which of the following would NOT be a sign of L2 difficulties in some students?
(Average) (Skill 9.6)

    A. expressive difficulties
    B. behavioral differences
    C. reading difficulties
    D. difficulties controlling emotions

Answer: D. difficulties controlling emotions
A, B, and C are all possible difficulties that ELLs experience while learning a L2. Difficulties in controlling emotions is not necessarily a L2 learning problem. Feelings of alienation and strangeness should diminish over the course of a school year. When they do not, it is a possible learning disorder. The correct answer is D.

104. Which piece of legislation listed below is NOT part of the Consent Decree compliance mandates?
(Average) (Skill 10.1)

    A. Requirements of Plyler v. Doe
    B. Section 504 of the Rehabilitation Act of 1973
    C. Equal Education Opportunities Act of 1974
    D. Title I (1965)

Answer: D. Title I (1965)
The correct answer is D. Title I provides funding to states to support extra assistance to students who need help in mathematics and reading. A, B, and C are parts of Florida's framework covered by the Consent Decree to comply with many federal and state laws and mandates regarding education.

105. The NCLB act of 2002, specifically focused on which of the following groups of children?
(Easy) (Skill 10.1)

    A. students aiming for college admission
    B. children overlooked by the educational system
    C. children of veterans
    D. children of single mothers

Answer: B. children overlooked by the educational system
The correct answer is B children often overlooked by the educational system including: children with disabilities, children from low-income families, non-English speaking children, and African American and Latino children.

106. According to the NCLB Act of 2002, which of the following statements is false?
   (Easy) (Skill 10.1)

   A. Standardized testing can be deferred one-time for one year, on a case-by-case basis for students receiving ESL services.
   B. Puerto Rican students may be exempt from taking standardized testing in English even if they have attended U.S. schools for 3 years.
   C. LEP students do not have to be included in all academic testing administered to other students.
   D. Tests are to be administered in the language most likely to provide accurate data of the LEP's academic achievement and performance.

Answer: C. LEP students do not have to be included in all academic testing administered to other students.
Answer C is the correct answer. Puerto Rican students are the exception to the rule that LEP students must receive tests administered in English after being in the school system for 3 years.

107. Which of the following tests would be administered by a school to determine how well an ELL understands the rules of punctuation?
   (Average) (Skill 10.2)

   A. a language placement test
   B. a language achievement test
   C. a language proficiency test
   D. a language diagnostic test

Answer: B. a language achievement test
A placement test is used to place a student within a specific program. A proficiency test is to determine if certain standards have been met in a particular language. A diagnostic test is used by speech therapists or psychologists in a clinical setting to determine if specific learning problems are present. To determine if specific goals of the curriculum have been achieved, a language achievement test is administered. The correct answer is B.

108. The TOEFL is which of the following types of tests?
   (Easy) (Skill 10.2)

   A. proficiency
   B. achievement
   C. diagnostic
   D. placement

Answer: A. proficiency
The TOEFL test is a proficiency test.

109. Why must language testing be done cautiously?
(Easy) (Skill 10.2)

    A. Tests are unreliable because they are not well prepared.
    B. Tests don't measure achievement.
    C. Language tests measure only a small portion of possible language dimensions.
    D. Language tests measure the wrong variables.

Answer: C. Language tests measure only a small portion of possible language dimensions.
Every effort is made to ensure that language tests measure what they purport to measure and that they are reliable. The correct answer is C. Language tests measure only about 12 of over 200 dimensions of a particular language.

110. In addition to Parent Leadership Councils (PLC), how does Florida inform parents about issues concerning their children?
(Easy) (Skill 10.3)

    A. through webpages
    B. issuing policy statements to the legislature
    C. sending home notices
    D. calling up parents

Answer: A. through webpages
The Florida Department of Education's Public Schools Division maintains webpages on different aspects of education for parents. The issuing of policy statements to the legislature would be of value for pending legislation. Sending home notices and calling up parents would be on the individual school level. The correct answer is A.

111. What is the role of the instructor when students are asked to provide self-assessment?
(Easy) (Skill 11.1)

    A. to provide the formats
    B. to encourage honesty
    C. to allow exaggeration
    D. to provide the criteria

Answer: D. to provide the criteria
Completely 'free' self-assessment would likely be of little use in evaluating most students. However, well-conducted self-assessment can't lead students to insights in where they are doing well and where they need to improve. By providing criteria and guidance, genuine assessment can be achieved. The correct answer is D.

112. Which one of the following is NOT a benefit of journals?
(Easy) (Skill 11.1)

A. ELLs gain additional writing practice.
B. Journals provide the teacher with an additional grade for each student.
C. Journals are useful for keeping records.
D. Journals are helpful in promoting an inner dialogue for the student.

Answer: B. Journals provide the teacher with an additional grade for each student.
Answers A, C, and D are benefits of journals. Journals should not be graded. Therefore, B is the correct answer.

113. In the language of testing, what is the definition of validity?
(Easy) (Skill 11.2)

A. a test that measures correct language
B. a test that measures test items accurately
C. accurate scoring of test items
D. a test which measures what it claims to measure

Answer: D. a test which measures what it claims to measure
A test which measures what it claims to measure is valid. D is the correct answer.

114. When an ELL demonstrates good oral skills in class, which of the following terms would an ESOL instructor expect to apply an oral proficiency test of the ELL?
(Average) (Skill 11.2)

A. concurrent validity
B. reliability
C. predictive validity
D. practicality

Answer: A. concurrent validity
Answer B refers to reliability or to similar scores when tests are retaken. Answer C refers to the possible outcomes of test performance. Answer D speaks of tests being accurate but possible unacceptable because of high costs or time consumption. Answer A is the correct choice. Concurrent validity occurs when a test variable is connected with another variable for measurement.

115. What is the value of alternative assessments?
(Easy) (Skill 11.3)

   A.   They are contextualized.
   B.   They are more structured.
   C.   Teacher observations are more accurate.
   D.   Teachers know more about how to test their own students.

Answer: A. They are contextualized.
Answers B, C, and D are possibly true in many cases. However, they do not provide the accuracy of well written standardized tests. Alternative assessments are valuable in that they are real-world and contextualized. The correct answer is A.

116. When evaluating a student during a story or text exercise, which of the following would a teacher be observing?
(Easy) (Skill 11.3)

   A.   the students reaction to the material
   B.   the interpretation of the material
   C.   response to the illustrations
   D.   written responses

Answer: A. the student's reaction to the material
In this type of evaluation, the instructor is mainly looking at the response of students to the text. Answer A is the correct response.

117. Why are rubrics a valuable way for ELLs to understand their problems?
(Average) (Skill 11.3)

   A.   Rubrics illustrate how the ELL compares with other students.
   B.   Rubrics compare the student with standardized testing.
   C.   Rubrics establish guidelines for a particular exercise or set of exercises.
   D.   Rubrics are good documentation for teachers.

Answer: C. Rubrics establish guidelines for a particular exercise or set of exercises.
Answers A and B are inaccurate because rubrics compare the student with standards for the work being evaluated. While rubrics may be a part of the documentation accumulated for an ELL in themselves, they are not documentation. Answer C is the correct answer.

118. What is one reason for teaching phrases such as 'Identify the main idea of the paragraph' and 'Circle the word which shows that means x' before a administering a standardized test?
(Average) (Skill 11.4)

    A.   teaches chunks of language
    B.   illustrates idioms for students
    C.   raises the affective filter
    D.   permits familiarity with the language of tests

Answer: D. permits familiarity with the language of tests
Answer A is true, but teaching chunks has little to do with administering a test. The phrases being taught are not idioms. If anything, being more familiar with the test should lower the affective filter, not raise it. The correct answer is D.

119. Which of the following techniques would be inappropriate to use when quickly checking for understanding of a reading passage?
(Average) (Skill 11.5)

    A.   give a timed quiz
    B.   ask a silly question
    C.   ask the student to retell the passage
    D.   focus on what is being communicated not the grammar

Answer: A. give a timed quiz
B, C, and D are all appropriate techniques to use to check for understanding. A timed quiz would probably frustrate ELLs who may not be familiar with timed exercises. The correct answer is A

120. When language errors interfere with understanding, what technique could an instructor use to correct the ELL without drawing attention to the error?
(Easy) (Skill 11.5)

    A.   explain why the language is incorrect
    B.   restate the question or sentence correctly
    C.   say ' I don't understand.'
    D.   make the learner restate his or her question or statement

Answer: B. restate the question or sentence correctly
The most beneficial way to correct simple errors is to ignore them and restate the question or statement correctly. B is the correct choice.

Interested in dual certification?

XAMonline offers over 25 FTCE study guides which are aligned to current standards and provide a comprehensive review of the core test content. Want certification success on your first exam? Trust XAMonline's study guides to help you succeed!

FTCE Series:

- **Educational Media Specialist PK-12**
  978-1-58197-578-9
- **Middle Grades General Science 5-9**
  978-1-60787-008-1
- **Middle Grades Social Science 5-9**
  978-1-60787-010-4
- **Exceptional Education Ed. K-12**
  978-1-60787-473-7
- **Guidance and Counseling PK-12**
  978-1-58197-586-4
- **Prekindergarten/Primary PK-3**
  978-1-60787-386-0
- **FELE Florida Education Leadership**
  978-1-60787-001-2
- **Elementary Education K–6**
  978-1-60787-506-2
- **FTCE Middle Grades English 5-9**
  978-1-58197-597-0
- **FTCE Physical Education K-12**
  978-1-58197-616-8

- **FTCE General Knowledge Test**
  978-1-60787-533-8
- **FTCE Mathematics 6–12**
  978-1-60787-505-5
- **FTCE Professional Education**
  978-1-60787-574-1
- **FTCE Social Science 6–12**
  978-1-60787-503-1
- **FTCE English 6-12**
  978-1-60787-463-8
- **FTCE ESOL K–12**
  978-1-60787-530-7
- **FTCE Biology 6-12**
  978-1-58197-689-2
- **FTCE Chemistry 6-12**
  978-1-58197-046-3
- **FTCE Physics 6-12**
  978-1-58197-044-9
- **FTCE Reading K-12**
  978-1-58197-659-5

Don't see your test? Visit our website: www.xamonline.com

XAMonline.com

CPSIA information can be obtained
at www.ICGtesting.com
Printed in the USA
BVOW07s1239220917

495635BV00017B/198/P